AVOIDANCE IS SUICIDE

The Truth We Are Afraid To Face

Anthoula Poulakos, PhD

This book is a work of nonfiction. The views and opinions expressed are solely those of the author and do not necessarily represent the views of any organization.

A Note to the Reader

This book was written for those who are tired of running from themselves. It is meant to be a companion on your path—a reminder that you are not alone in your pain, and that facing what you fear can lead to freedom. Move through these pages at your own pace. Take what resonates, pause when needed, and come back when you're ready. Healing is not a straight line, and there is no "right" way to do this work—only your way.

Trigger Warning

Within these pages, I share honest reflections and discussions around trauma, shame, abuse, and self-destructive behaviors. These topics may be activating or difficult to read. Please take care of yourself as you move through this book. Step back if you need to, breathe, and return when you feel ready. If at any point you feel overwhelmed, I encourage you to reach out for professional support.

Disclaimer

This book reflects the author's personal and professional perspectives on healing, trauma, and self-discovery. It is not a substitute for therapy, medical advice, or professional treatment. If you are experiencing significant emotional distress or crisis, please seek help from a qualified mental health professional.

"If you don't make the unconscious conscious, it will control you and you will call it fate."

— Carl Jung

To you.

May this book find you if you need it.

And may you finally come home to yourself.

To Quynh Lee and Kimberly Olson.

You believed in me and guided me back to my truth.

And to my dear mom, Pauline.

Though you are no longer here, your light is. I carry it with me, always.

TABLE OF CONTENTS

PREFACE

I was born in Brooklyn, New York, to a family of Greek descent. My parents made the difficult decision to move back to Greece, primarily because of my father, who wanted to return to Greece because he thought life would be better there. When I was three and a half years old, we left behind Brooklyn, New York, for a small town just outside Athens. Life in Greece started out as something my mother thought would bring stability, but my father left my mother not long after we arrived and returned to the US, where he stayed most of my childhood, apart from some short trips back and forth to visit. My brother and I were very young, and my mother was left raising us alone. Despite her strength and sacrifices, she stayed in a legal marriage out of fear—fear of losing what little stability we had. This decision was made to protect my brother and me, but it left her vulnerable to control and manipulation. My mother, despite the emotional and psychological pain, chose not to divorce him due to the threats he made. He convinced her that if they divorced, she would lose everything—properties, stability, any financial means of caring for her children. My mother stayed in a toxic, broken marriage for the sake of preserving some semblance of security. Little did she know, the true cost was much higher than any property or financial asset could ever represent.

But the trauma I experienced didn't only come from my mother and father's troubled marriage—it came from the very people who were supposed to protect me. By the age of four, I began experiencing a series of events that would shape my life in ways I could never have imagined. The people who should have been my protectors became my perpetrators—family members, family friends, and ultimately, my own biological father. Starting at the age of four, I was sexually abused by my cousin, who was in his teenage years at the time. It continued throughout my childhood, with instances of sexual abuse by my brother, followed by the son of family friends, and eventually, my own father. My father molested me when I was 5 years old and again when I was 8.

When I was 21 years old, my father drugged me and raped me. This time, I was no longer a child who could be easily manipulated into silence; however, I was unconscious after being drugged with a cup of tea, that was supposed to "relax me before bedtime." I thought my father was there to care for and protect me as he provided shelter and food for a time period while I was a college student. However, he was methodical, and his motives were completely different. He intended to drug me and rape me. I drank the tea he offered me on two occasions. The second time I woke up briefly and tried screaming but I felt like I had a sock or cotton in my mouth all the way down my throat and started choking and coughing instead. I felt unable to speak and like I was choking. The sensation lasted for a few minutes, and then I fell into deep sleep. I woke up the next morning with body odors and fluids and feeling like I was definitely violated. My left arm vein was bruised in the same way that it looks when you have a bad blood draw. My father was sounding anxious when he was knocking on my bedroom door, asking me to wake up. He was worried that he had done something irreversible and that maybe I wouldn't wake up. However, even though I woke up, the damage was irreversible and would stay with me for life.

That day, I had class, and I was part of a group project at my college. I remember walking towards the subway and contemplating what to do, and whether or not I should talk to anyone about what had happened. I remember passing by a hospital and contemplating going in there and telling them that I needed to get tested because I was raped. I recall my thought process and how all the shame and doubts kicked in. I recall reasoning myself out of going and choosing to do nothing instead and treat this as another day in college.

I remember thinking that I would not have anywhere to live and that I would be the cause of my family breaking apart. I remember thinking that my father would go to jail, and that somehow made me feel guilty and confused. I was so lost those minutes before choosing to hop on the subway and take the train to my school. I was alone and lost, and it was a terrible feeling. So, I buried it. I chose business as usual and silence. The silence lasted all the way until I started having sex on a regular basis with a boyfriend. The sensation brought back memories from childhood abuse. I rushed into therapy and for the first time ever in my life, spoke the words out loud that I had kept hidden all my life. At the time, I was 30 years old. Even though I remembered the first incident with my cousin, and the subsequent incidents with my brother and the son of childhood friends, at that time the memory of the rape from my father remained repressed until shortly before my mother passed away, when I struggled a lot with the onset of the memories that became conscious after my romantic partner at the time was waking me up in the middle of the night to have sex. I took myself to therapy, and two weeks later my mother passed away, never knowing what my father did to me. I confronted my father in adulthood, but my confrontation was met with denial. He told the rest of the family that I was "crazy," that I had fabricated the abuse in my mind. My brother sided with him and turned his back on me. Together, they rejected my truth and declared me crazy to the rest of my family, including my half-brother and his ex-wife and children, and my mother's sister.

Throughout my life, the relationship with my mother was tumultuous, but there was always love between us. However, I carried a lot of misdirected anger towards her. The anger towards my father was projected onto her, and I also felt a sense of betrayal from her for not protecting me. I was also angry at her for choosing him, for not divorcing him, and other things that rationally I was not always aware of. All of this was mostly unconscious until after she passed away, however, it colored every single interaction I had with her, even if it was a talk about the weather. With my mother gone, I was left to confront not just my father's actions, but the deep betrayal of my family. The loss of my mother cut even deeper than I could have ever imagined, and I had to live with the pain and the reality that I would not reconcile any of this with her or my father and brother. I lost my mother, and with her, the last semblance of a safety net.

The abuse went unchecked throughout all my life, and the silence was deafening. My mother never spoke to me or to anyone about what had happened to me, and the rest of the family continued to ignore it. They avoided acknowledging the truth, turning a blind eye to the pain I was enduring. It wasn't just that they failed to protect me—it was that they failed to comfort me when I needed them most. These events were buried deep within me, suppressed by shame and fear. When I finally tried to confront the truth, it was met with rejection, betrayal, and further trauma. Being that my brother had witnessed what my cousin had done to me, and he had in a couple of instances repeated it, it made sense that he would side with my father, because his identity, not only my father's identity, was also being threatened and he also could not cope with facing the truth.

I was in deep pain. It wasn't just the abuse I had suffered—it was the way my reality was twisted, my voice silenced. It was the gaslighting that made me question everything, and everyone, I had once trusted. The shame, guilt, and confusion I carried were not just the effects of the abuse itself, but also the consequences of being rejected and disbelieved by the very same people who had brought it on, the people that I once I loved and trusted the most, my own biological family members. At the same time, I was experiencing a similar element of being silenced at my workplace as a newly waivered psychologist, where the moment I chose to speak up and challenge mental health practices or even ask for clarification, I was shamed into silence. I felt triggered by this and alone, but I know now that the true challenge or the reason this was presenting was because I had to learn to trust myself. At the time, I did not have the words to process what I was feeling, or to explain it intellectually. I was in a deep state of loneliness and isolation. Furthermore, I was in a relationship that was part of my unhealed pattern, involving unavailable men and dynamics where confusion, shame, and guilt dominated. As I began to unwrap everything, my calling to write this book became stronger and stronger. I know that I am not alone. I know that you picked this book because you have also been in pain and looking for a way to heal. My story might be different than yours in terms of our background and the details. But it probably converges with yours when we begin to deconstruct how trauma thrives in darkness and how avoidance keeps us chained to our pain and erodes our self-worth until we are trapped in a vicious cycle, with seemingly no way out.

For years, I lived in avoidance—avoiding the truth of my past, the feelings it stirred, and the parts of myself that felt irreparably broken. This meant not becoming a therapist, and postponing facing my pain. It meant a series of failed relationships, with repeating patterns of toxic emotional dynamics. It meant over-reliance on myself. It meant avoiding vulnerability or closeness. It meant overintellectualizing things. Avoidance is not always a grand, obvious action. It is a slow, insidious process that chips away at our sense of self and our ability to experience life to its fullest. Often, it presents itself in subtle ways: the reluctance to confront uncomfortable feelings, the withdrawal from relationships, the perfectionism that keeps us from risking failure, or the self-sabotaging habits that prevent us from living fully. Over time, these avoidance behaviors accumulate, keeping us disconnected not just from our pain, but from the potential for deep healing and meaningful connection.

Avoidance is not living. It's a slow death, one that drains your soul and keeps you from becoming the person you're meant to be. This book is about my story, but it's also an invitation to you. To face what holds you back. To unmask the shadows. To awaken your true potential by confronting your pain, your fear, and, ultimately, yourself.

In Avoidance is Suicide, I explore the intricate relationship between trauma and avoidance, showing how this cycle ensnares us and keeps us trapped in patterns of fear, numbness, and disconnection. This book is an invitation to confront the most difficult truths about your internal struggles—the hidden wounds you attempt to bury—and the ways in which you unknowingly choose to disconnect from your fullest potential. The painful irony is that in trying to protect ourselves from the overwhelming emotions of trauma, we often inadvertently suffocate our own ability to heal, grow, and fully experience life. In the first chapter, "Trauma and the Shadows we Hide From", we examine the roots of trauma—how it forms, how it influences our perceptions, and how it affects the way we relate to our inner and outer world. We'll also explore the cycle of avoidance: how trauma compels us to evade the very feelings and experiences that are necessary for healing, ultimately creating a vicious cycle that traps us in fear and stagnation. This chapter will also focus on uncovering the hidden pain that fuels avoidance—those suppressed memories, unprocessed emotions, and unconscious patterns that continue to shape our actions without our awareness. Throughout the rest of this book, I hope to guide you through the process of recognizing, confronting, and ultimately dismantling the barriers of avoidance. We'll explore how to transform pain into growth, how to turn fear into courage, and how to begin the difficult but necessary work of facing the trauma that has shaped us. The journey will not be easy, but it is a journey of taking back your power—of reconnecting with yourself, embracing your vulnerabilities, and learning how to live authentically.

Avoidance is Suicide is not just a call to stop avoiding; it is a call to truly live. To choose to step into the discomfort, face the pain, and ultimately free yourself from the cycle that keeps you stuck. By doing so, you'll discover that life—though painful at times—offers far more than the illusion of safety that avoidance creates. Through this process of confronting and integrating your trauma, you will not only survive but learn to thrive. It is time to step out of the shadows of avoidance and into the fullness of life.

Writing this book is not my revenge; it is my reclamation. I am not here to humiliate, punish, or force anyone to accept me. I am here to hold a mirror to the patterns that once silenced me, so we can see them clearly and choose something better. If my words sting, it is because truth has a way of waking us up, not because I want to wound you, but because I refuse to let the wound keep running the show. The difference, and this is where it becomes healing instead of reenactment, is intention and delivery. When someone acts from unhealed rebellion, the goal is to punish, humiliate, or force acceptance through power. That is survival mode. With Avoidance is Suicide, the goal is to illuminate, liberate, and invite truth, even if it is uncomfortable for people to face. That is transformation mode. Through telling my story, I am still speaking to those who shamed, silenced, or dismissed me — but instead of swinging the sword wildly, I am laying it on the table and saying, Look. This is the blade you forged. I'm showing it to you so that others don't have to be cut by it. And this is the work of healing: to take back your voice, not so you can shout over others, but so you can finally hear yourself without the echo of shame. It is my wish that my voice and story will help you find and tell yours. Thank you for reading.

INTRODUCTION

Life, in its most profound sense, is a constant negotiation between pain and healing. Trauma is a universal experience that, in its many forms, can dramatically reshape the way we interact with ourselves, others, and the world. The intensity of trauma may differ, but its impact remains pervasive, often embedding itself into our thoughts, emotions, and behaviors. We run from what hurts, believing it offers relief and safety. However, avoidance—while protective in the short term—ultimately keeps us locked in a cycle of suffering. The true devastation does not lie in the trauma itself but in how we respond to it. When faced with overwhelming pain, we naturally turn to avoidance. Yet, this avoidance—while initially a defense mechanism—becomes a silent killer of our true selves; it strips us of our ability to fully engage with life and gradually robs us of our vitality. Unchecked, avoidance is a silent, slow form of self-destruction that can only be described as a quiet form of suicide.

The Child's Need for Approval: A Foundational Moment of Conformity

From the moment a child is born, they are deeply attuned to the approval and validation of their caregivers, particularly their parents, partly because they are dependent on their caregivers for immediate survival. A child's sense of worth is often framed by how they are seen, accepted, and loved by those who are entrusted with their care. In a healthy, nurturing environment, this need for approval can foster self-confidence, but in dysfunctional or conditional contexts, it breeds a deep reliance on external validation at the expense of authenticity. A child might suppress their own desires, preferences, or natural expressions—whether artistic, emotional, or intellectual—simply to receive love, safety, and recognition from their parent.

For example, if a child expresses an interest in something that does not align with the parent's values or expectations, they may experience rejection, disapproval, or indifference. To avoid this emotional pain, the child learns to suppress their authentic self and instead mirrors the parent's expectations, even if this results in a loss of individuality. Over time, this self-censorship becomes a coping mechanism—one that prioritizes the parent's approval over the child's internal desires and needs.

The Adult's Conformity to Societal Standards: A Continuation of the Childhood Dynamic

This pattern of seeking approval at the cost of authentic self-expression does not cease in childhood. As individuals grow into adulthood, the same need for external validation persists, but the focus shifts from parental approval to societal approval. The societal standards—such as success, beauty, productivity, or social acceptance—become the new "parental figure" parallel that the individual seeks to please, even at the expense of their true identity.

Just as the child learned to suppress their authentic self to gain parental love, the adult learns to suppress their individuality in order to meet the expectations of society. This conformity can take many forms: the pursuit of material success over emotional fulfillment, adherence to social norms that stifle personal creativity, or engaging in relationships based on social validation rather than genuine connection. The desire to fit in, to be accepted by the collective, drives the individual to mask their true desires and needs.

Just as the child may feel guilt, shame, or fear of rejection when they express a different opinion or act outside the bounds of their parents' expectations, the adult feels these same emotions when they diverge from societal standards. The individual internalizes the belief that their worth is contingent upon fitting into the mold prescribed by society and all its subsystems, which ultimately leads to a pervasive disconnection from their authentic self. The dynamic between a child seeking approval from a parent at the expense of self-expression and an adult conforming to societal standards at the expense of authenticity forms a crucial parallel in the cycle of shame, self-denial, and perpetuation of the status quo. Both scenarios represent a form of adaptive behavior where the individual's true self is subordinated to external validation—be it from a primary caregiver or the larger societal structure. The status quo depends on this unconscious subordination by the individual for its perpetuity. It turns out that those trapped by the system are the ones who end up prolonging it by engaging in the same behaviors that keep them stuck in it.

The Cycle of Shame, Self-denial, and Perpetuation of the Status Quo

When a child conforms to a parent's expectations to gain approval, they carry with them a distorted sense of self—one that is shaped more by external demands than internal truths. As this child grows into adulthood, the same pattern of external validation-seeking behavior continues, further entrenching the cycle of self-suppression. The individual's conformity to societal standards perpetuates the broader status quo: societal values, cultural norms, and external measures of success remain unquestioned and intact. By continuing to mask their authentic self, the individual contributes to the very systems of belief and behavior that oppress authenticity and self-expression.

The danger in this cycle is profound. Just as a child's relationship with their parent is formative in shaping their self-worth, society's collective values shape the individual's identity over time. Every act of conformity reinforces societal expectations, creating a feedback loop of shame and self-denial. The individual becomes complicit in upholding a system (and an image) that thrives on uniformity, performance, and the rejection of vulnerability.

The result is a world that prizes external validation over inner truth—a world where individuals are conditioned to suppress their authentic selves in favor of fitting into a narrow, predetermined set of standards. For the child who silences their true voice to gain a parent's love and then grows up to become an adult who silences their inner desires to gain societal approval, the pattern is the same: a disconnection from the self, perpetuated by the fear of rejection, disapproval, or nonconformity.

Breaking the Cycle: Reclaiming Authenticity

To break this cycle, the individual must learn to reconnect with their authentic self, to confront the shame that has been internalized both from their upbringing and from society. Just as the child must re-learn that their worth is not contingent upon their parent's approval, the adult must come to understand that their true value lies in their authenticity—not in the approval of others.

Healing requires self-acceptance, the willingness to embrace vulnerability, and the courage to reject societal norms that do not serve one's true self. It requires reclaiming one's voice, even if that voice has been suppressed for years in order to avoid pain or rejection. As we confront and heal the wounds created by our early experiences of approval-seeking, we begin to untangle the patterns that bind us to societal expectations.

By choosing authenticity over conformity, we can start to question the status quo. In doing so, we contribute to a broader collective shift—one that values self-expression, vulnerability, and personal truth over superficial success and external validation. Reclaiming our authenticity doesn't just heal us individually; it also has the potential to disrupt the very systems that perpetuate shame, avoidance, and disconnection from our true selves.

In the end, it's not about fitting into the mold that society dictates but about breaking free from that mold altogether. It's about returning to the essence of who we are and living in alignment with our own truth, regardless of the pressures to conform. The child who once sought approval from their parent, and the adult who now seeks approval from society, both have the power to heal and reclaim their authentic selves by choosing to prioritize their inner truth over external validation. The path to healing begins when we stop reshaping ourselves to fit a mold and, instead, embrace the fullness of who we truly are.

The Vicious Shaming Cycle: How External Comparison, Fear, Validation-Seeking, Ego, and Avoidance Enable the Status Quo

The human experience is often marked by a profound struggle between our authentic selves and the external forces that shape how we perceive our worth. This struggle frequently takes the form of a vicious cycle—a cycle that draws individuals into patterns of external comparison, fear-based thinking, validation-seeking behaviors, ego-driven actions, and avoidance. At its core, this cycle prevents healing, reinforces internalized shame, and sustains the societal structures that perpetuate disconnection from authentic self-expression. Arguably, this very same structure breeds mental illness. However, this is never talked about. The weight falls on the individual for not "functioning" as they should according to the set of societal and cultural, systemic standards that remain unquestioned.

1. External Comparison: The Seed of Shame

The shaming cycle begins with external comparison; a process deeply embedded in both societal norms and our individual experiences. From a young age, we are taught to measure our worth against others—whether it's in terms of appearance, success, wealth, or status. The pervasive influence of media, advertising, and social platforms exacerbates this comparison by constantly presenting idealized versions of success, beauty, and happiness that seem just out of reach.

When we compare ourselves to these external standards, we inevitably find ourselves lacking, and it is never-ending lack as long as it based on external comparisons. We see others as more successful, more attractive, or more fulfilled, which triggers feelings of inadequacy. This comparison becomes a breeding ground for shame—the sense that we are "not enough" in some fundamental way. We internalize these judgments, believing that our value is contingent on meeting these external standards. This self-judgment is the beginning of the vicious cycle, as it makes us feel "less than," fueling the need to seek validation from outside sources to compensate for our perceived inadequacies. It is not possible to heal without examining the roots of shame in our lives and the way it has shaped our view of self and others.

2. Fear-Based Mindset: The Reinforcement of Scarcity

The feelings of inadequacy generated by comparison give rise to a fear-based mindset. At the core of this mindset is the belief that we are not enough, and if we do not continually measure up to external standards, we risk rejection, failure, or abandonment. This fear keeps us trapped in a state of constant vigilance, where we are always striving to appear perfect, competent, and desirable. If I do x, they will do y. If I don't measure up, I will lose them, they will leave, I will be replaced, it means I am not good enough, something is wrong with me, I am unworthy, etc.

Fear becomes the engine that drives us to avoid uncomfortable emotions, especially the fear of being "exposed" or "found out" as unworthy or inadequate. It also drives the perpetual comparison game, as the mind constantly seeks to measure its own worth against others, creating a continuous cycle of stress, anxiety, and self-doubt. The fear of not being enough leads to a heightened sensitivity to perceived judgment, and the more we fear rejection or failure, the more we cling to external validation to soothe our anxieties.

3. The Need for Validation: Externalizing Self-Worth

In response to the feelings of inadequacy and fear, the need for validation emerges. This is the psychological mechanism by which we look to others for confirmation that we are worthy, successful, or lovable. The desire for external approval becomes a coping strategy to fill the void created by internal shame. Our actions then, are not fully chosen, based on our true values, but rather unconsciously dictated by the need for approval. We look for validation in relationships, achievements, social media approval, material success, and even in our appearance.

While seeking validation is a natural human instinct, when it becomes excessive and driven by the need to "prove" our worth to others, it becomes disempowering. We begin to attach our sense of self to the opinions and judgments of others, constantly seeking affirmation from external sources. This validation-seeking behavior becomes a trap—each time we receive approval, it only temporarily alleviates the deeper sense of emptiness and insecurity. In the absence of true internal validation, we are caught in an endless cycle of seeking affirmation without ever feeling truly seen or understood.

4. The Ego: The Guardian of the False Self

As this cycle of external validation continues, the ego becomes increasingly dominant. The ego, in its protective role, shields us from feelings of inadequacy by creating a false self—an identity constructed out of external achievements, roles, and validation. This false self is not an authentic reflection of who we truly are but rather a defensive mechanism designed to protect us from the pain of vulnerability and rejection.

The ego thrives on comparison, competition, and conformity because these factors reinforce its existence. It is through the ego that we measure ourselves against others and continually seek to bolster our self-worth through external approval. The ego's role is to defend us from perceived threats to our identity, but in doing so, it reinforces the very patterns that prevent true self-awareness and healing. The more we identify with the ego, the further we move away from our authentic selves.

Moreover, the ego fuels avoidance by creating defenses—walls, facades, and rationalizations—that keep us from confronting the deeper emotional truths that need healing. The ego convinces us that facing our true selves is too dangerous or painful, and thus we remain trapped in cycles of denial and superficiality.

5. Avoidance: The Masking of True Pain

Avoidance is the behavioral manifestation of this cycle. In order to protect ourselves from the overwhelming feelings of shame, fear, and inadequacy, we engage in various forms of avoidance. This might look like staying busy, overworking, numbing with substances, seeking distractions, or engaging in toxic relationships—all strategies to escape the discomfort of confronting our true emotional landscape.

The avoidance mechanism is particularly insidious because it is often cloaked in seemingly rational behaviors. For example, we might rationalize overworking as a way to achieve success or to be productive, while in reality, it is an attempt to avoid facing deeper emotional wounds, such as the fear of failure, rejection, or loss. Similarly, we may use social media or consumerism as a way to fill the void of inadequacy, while avoiding introspection and inner knowing by constantly seeking external validation. This book is an invitation to discover who we truly are underneath all of that.

Avoidance does not heal; it merely delays the inevitable confrontation with our inner pain. And in the long term, avoidance compounds the cycle of shame and fear, creating a deeper sense of disconnection from ourselves and from others. The longer we avoid confronting our true emotions, the more alienated we feel from our authentic selves, perpetuating a self-destructive cycle of avoidance and disempowerment.

6. Enabling the Status Quo: Reshaping and Reinforcing Social Norms

The cycle of external comparison, fear, validation-seeking, ego, and avoidance does not just remain individual—it is intimately tied to the broader societal context. In fact, this cycle enables the perpetuation of societal norms and values that prioritize conformity, external validation, and achievement at the expense of authenticity and self-expression.

When individuals continue to conform to societal expectations—seeking approval, chasing success, and avoiding vulnerability—they reinforce the status quo. The more we adhere to these externally imposed standards, the more we perpetuate a culture that devalues authenticity and emotional well-being. The cycle of comparison, fear, and avoidance becomes a feedback loop that keeps the collective stuck in a state of disconnection from their true selves.

This cycle also keeps us trapped in systems that thrive on maintaining the illusion of perfection, success, and productivity. Society's demand for constant performance and external achievement ensures that people remain disconnected from their core emotional truths. It is through the perpetuation of these ideals that social structures, such as the corporate world, consumer culture, and media, continue to exploit and manipulate individuals, keeping them trapped in cycles of comparison, fear, and avoidance.

Breaking the Cycle and Reclaiming Authenticity

To break this vicious cycle, we must first recognize its components: the external comparisons that fuel shame, the fear-based mindset that keeps us stuck, the validation-seeking behaviors that disempower us, the ego's control over our identity, and the avoidance strategies that numb us. Healing begins with awareness and the courage to step out of the cycle.

This means prioritizing inner validation over external approval, embracing vulnerability over perfection, and challenging the societal norms that encourage disconnection from our true selves. It requires a radical shift in perspective—one that values authenticity, self-compassion, and emotional openness above all else. Only by breaking free from the cycle of shame and avoidance can we begin to heal and reclaim our full potential as individuals, fostering a collective movement that values truth over conformity and healing over superficial success.

Understanding Avoidance: Defining Avoidance and Its Role in Self-Sabotage

Avoidance is more than just an emotional reaction; it is a deeply ingrained pattern of behavior that serves as a defense mechanism against pain, discomfort, or distressing memories. It manifests in many forms—disengagement from relationships, procrastination, numbing behaviors, or even physical withdrawal from situations that might trigger emotional vulnerability. At its core, avoidance is a strategy for short-term relief. When we avoid, we temporarily escape the distressing emotions that threaten to overwhelm us. But in doing so, we deny ourselves the opportunity to heal, grow, and process what we've been through.

This creates a vicious cycle. The more we avoid, the more our unresolved trauma and unprocessed shame fester in the unconscious, continuing to influence our behavior in subtle yet profound ways. This pattern of avoidance, which may initially appear as self-protection, is, in fact, a form of self-sabotage. Each time we avoid confronting our pain, we reinforce the belief that we are incapable of dealing with it, further distancing ourselves from our true selves and from the possibility of growth and healing.

The Illusion of Safety: Why Avoiding Pain Feels Safer but Leads to More Suffering

Avoidance presents itself as a refuge—a place where we can hide from our pain and experience temporary relief. The fear of facing difficult emotions, memories, or situations feels overwhelming, and so we choose the path of least resistance.

It seems safer to stay in the comfort of what we know, even if that comfort is an illusion. But the reality is that this false sense of safety comes at a high cost. The more we avoid, the more we become disconnected from our true selves, and the deeper we sink into the shadows of unresolved pain.

In the short term, avoidance may seem like a way to preserve emotional well-being. However, in the long run, it leads to greater suffering—both emotionally and physically. Unaddressed trauma seeps into our lives in ways we may not even recognize, contributing to feelings of anxiety, depression, irritability, and a sense of being "stuck." To counter these feelings, we drink, use drugs, overeat, undereat, lash out, get into fights, or start taking it out on ourselves by harming ourselves either overtly or covertly. The longer we avoid, the more entrenched these feelings become, creating a cycle that is harder and harder to break. Ultimately, the illusion of safety we cling to becomes a prison, one that keeps us from living fully and experiencing the richness of life.

The Urgency to Wake Up: How Avoidance Keeps You Stuck, and Why Now is the Time to Face What Holds You Back

Avoidance doesn't just keep us stuck in the past; it keeps us from fully participating in the present. The longer we evade confronting the truths of our experiences, the more difficult it becomes to move forward. What we fail to understand is that avoidance doesn't prevent the pain from existing—it merely keeps it buried beneath the surface, where it festers and influences us in hidden ways.

The urgency of waking up lies in the realization that avoiding pain only deepens the suffering. The time to face our fears, confront our trauma, and dismantle our avoidance behaviors is now. The longer we wait, the more the past controls us, and the more we lose access to the life we are meant to live.

Facing what we've been avoiding doesn't mean that we will instantly feel better or that the pain will vanish. It does mean, however, that we begin to take the first steps toward freeing ourselves from the chains that hold us in the past. This process of awakening is not easy, but it is necessary for transformation. We must stop running from what hurts and begin the challenging but deeply rewarding work of integrating our trauma, embracing our pain, and moving forward with the awareness and strength to truly heal.

Overview of the Book: Key Themes and How to Heal

This book is a journey through the core themes of trauma, shame, ego, avoidance, and self-worth. These themes are intricately interconnected, and each one plays a pivotal role in how we respond to pain and how we prevent ourselves from healing. Understanding these themes and becoming conscious of how they operate within us is the first step toward reclaiming our lives and our power.

Trauma: We begin by exploring what trauma truly is, how it shapes our thoughts, behaviors, and perceptions, and why it continues to influence us long after the event itself has passed.

Shame: Shame often emerges as a silent companion to trauma, a feeling of unworthiness that fuels avoidance and self-sabotage. We'll delve into how shame keeps us stuck and how we can begin to release its grip on our lives.

Ego: Our ego, often driven by fear and survival mechanisms, builds walls to protect us from emotional pain. But these defenses keep us disconnected from our true selves and prevent authentic healing. Learning to navigate and transcend the ego is key to breaking the cycle of avoidance.

Avoidance: As we've already discussed, avoidance is the primary mechanism by which we disconnect from our pain. We will look at how avoidance manifests in our lives and offer tools for gradually confronting and processing the emotional wounds we've been avoiding.

Self-Worth: At the heart of avoidance is often a deep sense of inadequacy or self-doubt. Reclaiming our self-worth is essential for healing. We will explore how to rebuild a healthy sense of self and break free from the patterns of self-rejection that have kept us stuck.

The key to healing these wounds lies in becoming conscious of them. Only when we acknowledge the ways in which trauma, shame, ego, and avoidance have shaped us can we begin to dismantle the barriers they've created. Through introspection, self-compassion, and actionable strategies, this book will guide you through the painful but essential process of confronting your deepest fears and releasing the behaviors that keep you trapped.

The journey ahead will not be easy, but it is necessary. Avoidance is Suicide is a call to action: to stop avoiding, to stop hiding, and to finally face what holds you back. By doing so, you will begin to reclaim your life, your power, and your true self. Now is the time to wake up, heal, and live fully.

CHAPTER 1

TRAUMA AND THE SHADOWS WE HIDE FROM

Trauma is not just what happens to us—it's how it stays with us, woven into the fabric of our minds and bodies. From the time I was four years old, the people who should have been my protectors became my perpetrators. My cousin. My brother. A family friend's son. And eventually, my own father. These violations shattered any sense of safety I had in the world. Each instance reinforced a belief I didn't have words for yet—that I was powerless, unworthy, and that silence was the only way to survive.

My survival mechanism was silence. I buried the pain deep within, trying to convince myself it hadn't happened or didn't matter. My family'avoidance mirrored my own. Conversations about the abuse were nonexistent, as if silence could erase what had occurred. But trauma doesn't disappear in silence. The perceptions that are born as a result of it, control us until we confront them head on. Trauma and its effects fester, manifest, and grow, shaping how we see ourselves and the world around us.

Trauma doesn't just happen to us—it reshapes us, embedding itself into the fabric of our thoughts, bodies, and relationships. It doesn't fade with time; it lingers, waiting for moments of vulnerability to remind us of its presence. And when we cannot face it, we do what feels like survival—we avoid.

For years, I lived in the shadows of avoidance. I told myself the past didn't matter, that I could move forward without revisiting the darkness. But avoidance is never a solution. It's a slow erosion of the self, a quiet unraveling that keeps us trapped in cycles of fear, self-doubt, and pain.

I buried the pain so deep that it wasn't at the forefront of my memory anymore. No one talked about what had happened, and so, I learned that silence was the price of belonging. But trauma ends up creeping up into the way we see ourselves, the choices we make, and the way we show up in the world.

I didn't recognize the extent of the damage until later in life. It wasn't just the memories that haunted me—it was the way they shaped my relationships, my self-worth, and my ability to trust. I found myself in dynamics that echoed the past, unconsciously drawn to situations that reinforced my deepest fears. The unhealthy dynamics that seemed familiar were mistaken for belonging, and far more tolerated than they should have been. In my life, the avoidance of facing what had happened to me was a survival mechanism, but in the long run, it was killing me. Since trauma reinforces feelings of shame, guilt and self-doubt, we continue to seek approval from similar unhealthy dynamics to numb these effects. We stay because if we leave, it means something is wrong with us. We stay because something in us says, if I heal this dynamic, maybe I am worthy after all. Maybe I am good enough for sticking it out. If I leave it means I have to heal, it means I have to confront my choices and their origins. Sometimes it's scarier to do that than to stay in the unhealthy dynamic. The truth is, avoiding pain doesn't free us from it—it binds us to it. And for those of us who have endured trauma, avoidance can feel like the only option. But what if the very thing we are running from is the key to our liberation? Eventually, we will come to realize that only we can give to ourselves the validation, approval and whatever else we are seeking from unhealthy dynamics.

The Cycle of Trauma and Avoidance

Trauma, at its core, is an injury to the mind, body, and spirit. It is not just about what happens—it's about how it gets stored within us, how it shapes our responses, and how it dictates the ways we engage with the world.

The brain is designed to protect us from harm, but when trauma occurs, our nervous system often becomes stuck in survival mode. We may develop hypervigilance, dissociation, or emotional numbing—all ways the mind and body attempt to shield us from further pain. But these mechanisms come at a cost.

Hypervigilance keeps us constantly on edge, scanning for danger even in safe spaces.

Dissociation numbs us, disconnecting us from our own emotions and experiences.

Emotional numbing helps us avoid pain but also strips us of joy, love, and connection.

The more we avoid, the deeper the wounds fester. Avoidance doesn't heal—it prolongs. It keeps us from facing the truth, from confronting the pain that needs to be processed in order to move forward.

But how do we break this cycle? How do we face the very thing we've spent years running from?

Stepping Into Awareness

Healing begins the moment we become conscious of what we've been avoiding. It is in naming the pain, in allowing ourselves to feel, that we reclaim our power. The journey is not about reliving trauma—it's about acknowledging its presence and choosing, day by day, to confront it instead of burying it deeper. Avoidance is not living. It is an existence dictated by fear, a slow suffocation of the soul. But facing what we fear is the first step toward reclaiming ourselves. The shadows we hide from do not disappear when we refuse to look at them. They grow. They spread. And they hold us captive. But when we turn to face them—when we stop running—we begin the journey back to ourselves. So, if I am for example convinced inside of me that I am "not good enough," what will I do to numb that feeling so that I can feel worthy? And at what cost? And if I keep trying to prove myself worthy, is this truly living? Am I truly choosing life from that state?

The Roots of Trauma

Trauma is a multifaceted psychological and physiological phenomenon, encompassing both individual and collective experiences that disrupt an individual's sense of safety, identity, and well-being. It manifests not merely as isolated events but as enduring disruptions in cognitive, emotional, and somatic processes. It is characterized by a profound rupture in an individual's ability to integrate experience, often resulting in long-term psychological and physiological consequences.

Traumatic events—ranging from interpersonal violence to natural disasters, or even subtle, chronic forms of neglect and emotional invalidation—interfere with the natural developmental processes that guide healthy coping mechanisms, self-regulation, and emotional resilience. These experiences imprint themselves on the psyche, influencing how individuals perceive themselves, others, and the world around them. Trauma, therefore, is not confined to the event itself but extends into how it is internalized, processed, and embodied over time. Cognitive distortions—such as a pervasive sense of unworthiness, shame, or distrust—emerge as survival mechanisms that further entrench the individual in maladaptive ways of relating to both internal and external stimuli.

Trauma shapes the neural architecture of the brain, particularly in regions involved in emotional processing, memory, and executive functioning. The hippocampus, amygdala, and prefrontal cortex are particularly affected, leading to disruptions in memory consolidation, emotion regulation, and decision-making abilities. Consequently, individuals may experience hypervigilance, dissociation, or emotional numbing, all of which serve as protective mechanisms to avoid re-experiencing the overwhelming emotions and bodily sensations associated with trauma.

1. Hippocampus (Memory and Learning)

The hippocampus is critical for forming and retrieving explicit memories. Trauma, especially prolonged stress, can lead to hippocampal atrophy due to chronic cortisol exposure. This shrinkage can cause impaired memory, difficulty distinguishing between past and present (common in PTSD flashbacks), and problems differentiating between real and perceived threats. Neurogenesis in the hippocampus is also inhibited, making recovery from trauma more difficult.

2. Amygdala (Fear and Emotional Processing)

The amygdala is responsible for processing emotions, particularly fear and threat detection. Trauma hyperactivates the amygdala, leading to an exaggerated fear response and heightened emotional reactivity. This can result in increased anxiety, hypervigilance, and difficulty regulating emotional responses. Since the amygdala and hippocampus work together to encode memories, a dysregulated amygdala can make traumatic memories feel vivid and intrusive.

3. Prefrontal Cortex (Rational Thinking and Impulse Control)

The prefrontal cortex (PFC) is responsible for executive function, impulse control, and emotional regulation. Trauma reduces activity and connectivity in the PFC, leading to difficulty in logical reasoning, emotional regulation, and impulse control. A weakened PFC makes it harder to override amygdala-driven fear responses, contributing to reactivity, poor decision-making, and difficulty calming down after stress.

The Overall Effect

The overactive amygdala (fear), underactive PFC (rational control), and damaged hippocampus (memory processing) create a cycle where traumatic memories feel ever-present, emotions are hard to regulate, and rational decision-making is impaired. This neural imbalance contributes to symptoms of PTSD, anxiety, and emotional dysregulation. Healing from trauma involves rebuilding neural connections, often through therapy (e.g., EMDR, CBT), mindfulness, meditation, and somatic practices.

The Cycle of Avoidance

The relationship between trauma and avoidance is central to understanding the persistence and exacerbation of psychological distress. In the aftermath of traumatic experiences, individuals frequently resort to avoidance behaviors as a means of managing emotional and sensory overload. These behaviors, which can manifest in physical withdrawal, dissociation, or cognitive avoidance, initially serve as protective strategies, enabling individuals to shield themselves from further psychological harm. However, this avoidance paradoxically reinforces the trauma, creating a cyclical pattern that perpetuates the individual's suffering.

The cycle of avoidance is self-reinforcing. By steering clear of situations, thoughts, or memories that evoke distressing emotions, individuals inadvertently prevent themselves from confronting and processing their trauma. This leads to the entrenchment of the trauma in the unconscious mind, where it continues to influence thoughts, behaviors, and perceptions in subtle but pervasive ways. The avoidance not only blocks access to emotional healing but also impedes cognitive restructuring—the process by which individuals can reinterpret traumatic events in a way that allows for greater psychological integration and meaning-making.

Over time, avoidance can expand, encompassing not only specific triggers but also broader aspects of life. This may result in the individual withdrawing from social relationships, professional opportunities, or even engagement with everyday activities. The avoidance, initially a coping strategy, becomes a prison, reinforcing isolation, shame, and helplessness, and further embedding the trauma in the individual's lived experience.

Uncovering Hidden Pain

The process of uncovering suppressed trauma requires a delicate balance of safety, self-compassion, and introspection. Unresolved trauma is often stored in the unconscious mind, manifesting through subtle emotional and physiological cues that may not be immediately accessible to the conscious self. These suppressed memories and feelings exert a quiet yet pervasive influence on behavior, frequently leading to maladaptive patterns such as chronic anxiety, depression, or self-sabotage. This can manifest into poor eating, sleeping, drinking habits as well as escapism tendencies (i.e., gambling, promiscuity, drug use, etc.)

To bring unconscious trauma into conscious awareness, individuals must develop a willingness to explore the emotional landscapes they have long sought to avoid. This can involve revisiting memories that have been repressed or dissociated, often through therapeutic modalities such as guided imagery, trauma-informed psychotherapy, or somatic experiencing. By learning to identify and decode the implicit messages encoded in bodily sensations, emotional reactions, and intrusive thoughts, individuals can begin to unlock the underlying pain that drives their avoidance behaviors.

Critical to this process is the concept of psychological safety. Trauma survivors often experience a pervasive sense of mistrust, not only toward others but also toward themselves and their emotional responses. Creating a sense of safety—whether through supportive relationships, therapeutic alliances, or self-compassionate practices—enables individuals to confront and process these hidden wounds without retraumatizing themselves. The goal is not simply to recall painful memories but to integrate them into a coherent narrative that allows for healing, growth, and resilience.

Practical Exercise: Journaling Prompts to Uncover Trauma and Identify Avoidance Patterns

Engaging in a reflective journaling practice can be an invaluable tool in uncovering suppressed trauma and identifying patterns of avoidance. Writing facilitates the externalization of internal experiences, making it easier to observe and analyze one's thoughts and emotions from a more detached perspective. Below are a series of journaling prompts designed to help you explore and identify areas where trauma may be impacting your life and how avoidance patterns may be reinforcing emotional pain. Through this process, the hope is to gradually replace avoidance with acceptance, integration, and self-compassion, allowing for a deeper connection with both your past and your present.

1. Reflect on a traumatic event or series of events in your life: What emotions surface when you think about this experience? Are there any memories or details that are difficult to access? How do you feel in your body when you recall this event?
2. Identify patterns of avoidance: What situations, people, or activities do you tend to avoid? How do these avoidance behaviors manifest in your daily life? What emotions or thoughts do you associate with these avoidance tendencies?
3. Explore the physical sensations tied to avoidance: When you engage in avoidance, do you notice any changes in your body? Do you feel tension, numbness, or discomfort? How do these bodily sensations inform your emotional state?
4. Examine the impact of avoidance on your relationships: In what ways have your avoidance behaviors influenced your relationships with others? Have you noticed any patterns of withdrawal, isolation, or difficulty connecting with others?
5. Reflect on your self-talk: What do you tell yourself about the traumatic events in your life? How does this internal

dialogue contribute to your avoidance? Are there any self-critical or self-judging thoughts that reinforce your reluctance to confront pain?

6. Consider the role of shame and guilt: How do feelings of shame or guilt manifest in your avoidance? Do you find yourself believing that you are unworthy of healing or that confronting your trauma will make things worse?
7. Visualize healing and growth: Imagine what it would feel like to release the grip of trauma and avoidance. What would your life look like if you could embrace your pain with compassion? What steps could you take, however small, to begin moving toward healing?

CHAPTER 2

THE RELATIONSHIP BETWEEN SHAME AND TRAUMA: HOW SHAME IS OFTEN A BYPRODUCT OF TRAUMA AND HOW IT KEEPS YOU IN AVOIDANCE

If trauma is the wound, shame is the infection that keeps it from healing. It seeps into our bones, whispering that we are unworthy, broken, beyond repair. Shame is different from guilt. Guilt says, "I did something bad." Shame says, "I am bad." It convinces us that what happened to us reflects who we are. That we deserved it. That we were complicit. That we are too damaged to be loved. And eventually, we begin to embody that in terms of our actions and choices.

For years, I carried shame like a second skin. It dictated my choices, my relationships, my sense of self-worth. I was unconsciously drawn to people who reinforced my deepest fear—that I was not enough. That I did not deserve love or respect. That betrayal was inevitable. I found myself in relationships that mimicked the past, with dynamics that reinforced the belief that love meant longing, that I would always be the one reaching for someone who wouldn't reach back.

At the time, I couldn't see the pattern. I thought these relationships were fate, when in reality, they were reflections of my unhealed wounds. I was seeking validation from people who were just as broken as I was, hoping that if I could make them love me, I could somehow erase the shame I carried. Needless to say, maybe they were fated too, because without them, I would not have reached the level of awareness that I am describing.

The Weight of Shame and the Lies It Tells Us

Shame convinces us of many things:

- That we are unworthy of real love.
- That if people saw our true selves, they would leave.
- That we must earn our worth through performance, perfection, compliance, or self-sacrifice.
- That our pain is a burden, and we should carry it alone.

But shame is a liar. And the more we avoid it, the more power it gains.

Breaking Free from Shame

The only way to release shame is to bring it into the light. Shame thrives in secrecy and silence, but it cannot survive exposure. When we name it, when we speak our truth, when we allow ourselves to be seen shame begins to lose its grip.

Healing from shame means:

- Acknowledging its presence—recognizing the ways it has shaped our choices and self-perception.
- Challenging the narrative—questioning the beliefs that shame has ingrained in us.
- Allowing ourselves to be seen—by safe people, by ourselves, without judgment.

I won't lie—this process is painful. There were moments when confronting my shame felt unbearable. But on the other side of that pain was freedom. The moment I stopped apologizing for my existence, the moment I stopped trying to prove my worth to those who couldn't see it—I began to heal. The truth is, we were never meant to carry shame alone. And we were never meant to be defined by the things that happened to us. Our worth is not up for debate. It never was.

Shame is a deeply ingrained emotional experience that arises from the perception of having violated internalized standards or societal norms. It is distinct from guilt, in that while guilt is the recognition of having done something wrong, shame reflects a perceived deficiency in the self—it is the feeling of being fundamentally flawed. In the context of trauma, shame often becomes an integral byproduct of the traumatic experience, compounding the emotional wounds that trauma inflicts. While trauma involves an event or series of events that disrupt one's sense of safety and well-being, shame emerges as a corrosive response that reinforces feelings of powerlessness, unworthiness, and defectiveness.

Trauma and shame are often inextricably linked, with trauma creating fertile ground for the development of shame-based beliefs. For example, individuals who have experienced interpersonal violence, neglect, or emotional invalidation may internalize messages of inferiority or undesirability, assuming the trauma was a reflection of their own inadequacy. In this way, the trauma does not simply remain as an isolated event, but becomes intertwined with the individual's self-concept, leading to the pervasive feeling that something is wrong with them at a core level. This distorted self-image, forged in the crucible of trauma, becomes a significant driver of avoidance behavior. To avoid further reinforcing the shame associated with the trauma, individuals may withdraw, disengage, or perpetuate self-destructive habits that maintain the psychological distance from the pain. In essence, shame becomes both a product and a perpetuator of trauma, entrenching the individual in cycles of avoidance that prevent healing and growth.

The relationship between trauma and shame is not purely psychological but is deeply somatic as well. The body registers shame in visceral ways—through tension, fatigue, or a generalized sense of discomfort—and these bodily sensations are often avoided or suppressed, further embedding the experience of shame in the unconscious mind. In this way, the avoidance of emotional and somatic cues of shame can further entrench individuals in trauma responses, maintaining a cycle of disconnection and self-rejection.

Shame and Self-Worth: The Impact of Shame on Your Sense of Self-Worth and How It Undermines Your Confidence

Shame profoundly impacts an individual's sense of self-worth, often leading to a fragile and diminished view of oneself. This impaired self-worth is rooted in the belief that one is fundamentally unworthy of love, respect, or success. Shame-based individuals often perceive themselves as unlovable or defective, and as a result, they may feel a constant need to prove their worth, both to themselves and to others. This need for validation, however, is often futile, as shame operates from a place of deep insecurity that can never be fully assuaged through external approval or achievement.

The internalization of shame undermines the individual's confidence in several key ways. First, it erodes their ability to engage authentically with others. Fear of being exposed or judged often leads to emotional withdrawal and self-protective behaviors, such as excessive people-pleasing, perfectionism, or avoidance of vulnerability. The constant concern with how one is perceived by others can result in a hyper-focus on maintaining a façade of competence or success, rather than fostering genuine, self-affirming interactions. This disconnection from authentic self-expression further perpetuates the cycle of shame, as the individual is never able to truly experience acceptance—either from others or from themselves.

Moreover, the internalized voice of shame becomes a critical inner dialogue, often taking the form of negative self-talk that reinforces feelings of inadequacy. Statements like "I am not enough," "I am broken," or "I am unworthy" become internalized truths that shape an individual's behavior, limiting their potential and capacity for self-compassion. This self-rejection creates barriers to self-empowerment and achievement, as individuals may self-sabotage or avoid opportunities that might challenge their negative self-concept. In this way, shame is not simply an emotional experience but a pervasive force that warps the individual's relationship with themselves, others, and the world. The damage caused by shame is long-lasting, often requiring a concerted effort to reframe the negative beliefs about the self and to build a healthier, more resilient sense of self-worth.

The Lie of Perfection: How Shame Perpetuates the Need to Appear Perfect, Which Fuels Avoidance

One of the most insidious byproducts of shame is the belief in the need for perfection. Perfectionism, often fueled by a deep fear of rejection or exposure, becomes a defense mechanism against the intolerable feeling of being "not enough." For individuals who struggle with shame, the need to appear perfect is a means of guarding against judgment, both from others and from oneself. Perfectionism promises an illusion of safety—the idea that if we can control every aspect of our appearance, behavior, and performance, we can avoid the pain of feeling inadequate or unworthy.

However, the pursuit of perfection is inherently self-defeating. The standards of perfection are impossible to meet, and when individuals inevitably fall short, they are left with an even deeper sense of shame and self-rejection. The more one tries to attain perfection, the more elusive it becomes, perpetuating a vicious cycle of striving, failing, and hiding. This perfectionistic drive often leads to chronic dissatisfaction and burnout, as well as heightened anxiety and stress. The focus on perfection also fuels avoidance, as individuals seek to shield themselves from situations where they may not measure up or where their imperfections might be exposed.

Rather than fostering growth or self-acceptance, the pursuit of perfection deepens the grip of shame, reinforcing the belief that one must always appear flawless to be worthy of love or respect. This constant striving for an unattainable ideal prevents individuals from experiencing the freedom of imperfection, and in turn, it keeps them trapped in patterns of avoidance, self-criticism, and emotional paralysis.

Healing Shame: Steps to Unravel Shame and Reclaim Your Self-Worth Through Self-Compassion and Acceptance

The journey toward healing is not about eradicating shame entirely but about changing the way we relate to it, transforming it from a source of self-judgment into a catalyst for self-awareness and growth. Healing from shame requires a multifaceted approach that involves unraveling the negative self-beliefs that have been internalized and cultivating a deeper sense of self-compassion.

1. Awareness and Acceptance: The first step in healing shame is recognizing and accepting its presence. Shame often thrives in secrecy and denial, so it is crucial to bring it into conscious awareness. This involves acknowledging the emotions and memories that elicit feelings of shame and allowing oneself to feel those emotions without judgment. Acceptance of those emotions does not mean approval; it simply means allowing the emotions to exist without attempting to suppress or avoid them.

2. Self-Compassion: Cultivating self-compassion is a critical aspect of healing shame. This involves treating oneself with the same kindness and understanding that one would offer to a friend who is suffering. Self-compassion requires replacing harsh self-criticism with a nurturing inner dialogue. Instead of internalizing messages of inadequacy, individuals must learn to speak to themselves in ways that are affirming, gentle, and supportive.
3. Reframing the Inner Critic: The inner critic that fuels shame must be identified and reframed. This requires confronting the negative beliefs that have been internalized and actively challenging them. For example, shifting from "I am unworthy" to "I am deserving of love and respect, even with my imperfections" can gradually dismantle the power of shame. Over time, this reframing allows individuals to rewrite their internal narrative, replacing self-rejection with self-acceptance.
4. Reconnecting with Authenticity: Healing shame also involves reconnecting with one's authentic self. This means embracing imperfections, allowing vulnerability, and engaging in activities that foster a sense of true connection—both with others and with oneself. By stepping away from the façade of perfection, individuals

can reclaim their inherent worthiness and feel liberated from the need to hide or perform.

Practical Exercise: Creating a Self-Love Affirmation Practice to Counteract Shame-Based Thinking

One effective way to combat shame is through the practice of self-love affirmations. These affirmations are designed to counteract the negative, shame-based thoughts that often arise, replacing them with positive, affirming beliefs about oneself. The practice of regularly reciting these affirmations helps rewire the brain and cultivate a healthier, more compassionate self-view. Through this exercise, you can begin to dismantle the grip of shame and replace its influence with the empowering force of self-love and acceptance. Healing shame is not a linear process, but with patience and practice, it is possible to reclaim your self-worth and step into a more authentic, fulfilled version of yourself.

1. Write Down Your Affirmations: Begin by identifying the key areas where you feel the most shame or self-doubt. For example, if you struggle with feelings of unworthiness, an affirmation might be, "I am worthy of love and respect just as I am." If you struggle with perfectionism, an affirmation could be, "I am enough, even in my

imperfections." Write down at least five affirmations that resonate with you.

2. Daily Practice: Set aside time each day—preferably in the morning or before bed—to recite your affirmations aloud or silently. As you say each affirmation, allow yourself to feel the truth behind the words. Visualize yourself embodying the qualities of love, worth, and acceptance that the affirmations represent.
3. Reflect and Adjust: Over time, reflect on how your feelings of shame and self-worth evolve. Notice if any negative thoughts or beliefs begin to shift. Adjust your affirmations as needed to address new areas of growth or self-compassion.

CHAPTER 3

THE EGO'S ROLE IN AVOIDANCE

The Ego as Protector: Understanding the Ego's Role in Defending You from Perceived Emotional Threats

The ego, as a psychological construct, functions as a critical mediator between the individual's sense of self and the external world. Derived from the Greek/Latin word for "I," the ego serves as the subjective "I" or "me" in both conscious and unconscious processes. It is responsible for organizing and interpreting sensory input, managing one's identity, and ensuring psychological coherence within the context of the social environment. However, while the ego plays an essential role in helping individuals navigate daily life, its role in protecting the self can become maladaptive, particularly when it perceives emotional threats.

At its core, the ego is designed to protect the individual from harm, both physical and psychological. This protective function emerges from the ego's identification with the self-preservation instinct, which seeks to minimize vulnerability, discomfort, and perceived danger. In the context of trauma or unresolved emotional wounds, the ego becomes hyper-vigilant, interpreting any potential source of pain or discomfort as a threat to the integrity of the self. This heightened sensitivity to emotional threats leads to the creation of defensive mechanisms aimed at avoiding or warding off those perceived dangers.

These defense mechanisms—such as denial, repression, projection, and rationalization—are unconscious strategies employed by the ego to maintain psychological stability in the face of emotional turmoil. For example, a person who has experienced significant rejection or abandonment may develop a defense mechanism in the form of emotional withdrawal or detachment from relationships, thus preventing further pain. While these mechanisms may offer temporary relief from distress, they often serve to entrench avoidance patterns, keeping the individual stuck in a cycle of emotional disconnection and stagnation.

The ego's protective functions, though initially adaptive, can inadvertently prevent individuals from engaging in the healing processes necessary to transcend trauma and emotional suffering. Instead of confronting uncomfortable emotions or confronting the root causes of pain, the ego encourages avoidance behaviors that maintain the illusion of safety. Over time, these avoidance strategies create a false sense of stability, preventing growth, self-awareness, and deeper emotional integration.

Ego's Fear of Discomfort: Why the Ego Resists Change, Growth, and Facing Uncomfortable Truths

The ego's resistance to change and growth is rooted in its primary function of maintaining psychological equilibrium. This function is not inherently negative, as the ego strives to preserve the individual's sense of self and minimize feelings of insecurity. However, the ego operates from a fear-based framework, primarily motivated by the desire to avoid discomfort, uncertainty, and perceived threats to one's self-image. This fear of discomfort is a central reason why the ego resists personal growth, transformation, and the confrontation of uncomfortable truths.

When the ego perceives any change as potentially destabilizing or threatening to its established identity, it actively seeks to avoid such changes. This resistance is often experienced as an internal struggle between the desire for growth and the pull to remain within familiar, albeit limiting, patterns. For instance, a person who has spent years avoiding difficult emotions may be faced with the choice to confront those feelings in order to heal. However, the ego's aversion to discomfort prompts an instinctive pull to retreat into avoidance, even if this choice perpetuates suffering in the long run.

This dynamic is compounded by the ego's attachment to familiar identities and self-concepts. The ego resists anything that challenges its established view of the world and the self, even if doing so would lead to greater fulfillment. The fear of discomfort is thus tied to the ego's fear of losing control, fear of failure, and fear of exposing vulnerabilities. Facing uncomfortable truths or embarking on personal growth means risking the dissolution of long-held beliefs, identities, and defenses that the ego has built to protect the self from perceived harm.

However, this resistance to discomfort is paradoxical. The very growth that the ego fears is often the key to healing and breaking free from the cycles of avoidance. True personal transformation requires moving through discomfort, embracing vulnerability, and challenging the limitations that the ego has placed on one's sense of self. By resisting change, the ego perpetuates a state of stagnation, keeping the individual in a perpetual state of avoidance, self-protection, and emotional paralysis.

The Mask We Wear: How the Ego Creates False Identities to Protect Us from Pain, Leading to Further Avoidance

In its attempt to shield the self from emotional pain, the ego constructs elaborate false identities, or masks, that serve to deflect discomfort and maintain an appearance of emotional invulnerability. These masks are often a direct response to perceived inadequacies, fears of rejection, or unresolved trauma. The ego creates these masks to project a version of the self that appears more competent, confident, or "acceptable" to the outside world, thus protecting the individual from criticism, judgment, or the vulnerability of showing one's true self.

For example, a person who has experienced significant emotional neglect as a child might develop a mask of overachieving perfectionism, constantly striving to meet external standards of success to gain validation and avoid feelings of unworthiness. Similarly, someone who has suffered emotional betrayal may create a mask of emotional detachment or stoicism, hiding vulnerability to protect against future hurt. These false identities are not inherently malicious, but are adaptive responses to deep-seated emotional pain; yet they only serve to deepen the individual's sense of disconnection from their authentic self.

The problem with these masks is that they are inherently limiting and unsustainable. By constructing an identity that is not rooted in genuine self-awareness, the individual becomes increasingly disconnected from their true desires, needs, and values. This disconnection perpetuates avoidance, as the ego continues to prioritize self-protection over self-realization. The longer these false identities are maintained, the more difficult it becomes for the individual to distinguish between who they truly are and who they are pretending to be. The ego's desire to avoid pain leads to the adoption of identities that ultimately lead to greater emotional dissonance and personal fragmentation.

Moreover, these masks can create a façade of control, success, or emotional stability, but underneath this surface lies an unconscious, unresolved sense of unworthiness and fear. The ego, in its attempt to avoid emotional vulnerability, prevents the individual from engaging with their deeper, more authentic self. This further entrenches avoidance behaviors, as the individual becomes increasingly consumed by the need to protect the mask, rather than confront the raw and uncomfortable emotions hidden beneath it.

Shifting from Ego to Soul: How to Move from Ego-Driven Behavior to Authentic, Soul-Driven Choices

Shifting from ego-driven behavior to soul-driven choices involves a fundamental transformation in the way we relate to ourselves and the world. The ego, driven by fear, self-protection, and external validation, leads us into patterns of avoidance that limit personal growth and true connection. The soul, in contrast, represents the deeper, authentic self—the aspect of us that is aligned with truth, compassion, and purpose. Moving from the ego to the soul requires a conscious effort to transcend the defensive behaviors of the ego and reconnect with the essence of who we are beneath the masks we wear.

This shift involves several key components:

1. Self-Awareness: Becoming aware of the ego's patterns of behavior is the first step toward transcending them. This requires observing the ways in which the ego deflects discomfort, fear, and vulnerability, and understanding how these patterns have influenced one's choices. By recognizing these behaviors as ego-driven, we can begin to loosen their grip and create space for more authentic responses.
2. Embracing Vulnerability: One of the core aspects of soul-driven behavior is the willingness to embrace vulnerability. While the ego shields us from discomfort, the soul invites us to engage with life authentically, even when it feels uncomfortable. Vulnerability is the gateway to healing, growth, and true connection, and it requires the courage to step into the unknown, free from the need for external validation.
3. Living in Alignment with Values: Soul-driven choices are aligned with our deepest values and sense of purpose. These choices come from a place of internal guidance, rather than external expectations. To make soul-driven decisions, it is necessary to cultivate clarity around what

truly matters and to allow these values to guide one's actions, rather than the ego's need for control or approval.

4. Letting Go of Perfection: The ego thrives on perfectionism, but the soul thrives on authenticity. Shifting from ego to soul means letting go of the need to appear flawless and embracing the beauty of imperfection. By releasing the grip of perfectionism, individuals create space for self-compassion, vulnerability, and true self-expression.

Practical Exercise: Identifying the False Identities You Have Adopted and Writing a New, More Authentic Self-Description

A practical exercise for shifting from ego-driven behavior to soul-driven choices involves identifying the false identities that the ego has created as defense mechanisms. These identities may have served a protective purpose at one time, but they no longer align with your authentic self. The exercise is designed to help you reconnect with who you truly are beneath these masks and rewrite your self-description in a way that reflects your true essence. By identifying and shedding the false identities created by the ego, you begin the transformative process of shifting from avoidance and protection to authenticity and self-realization. This journey requires courage and self-awareness, but it is essential for breaking free from the cycles of avoidance and reclaiming your true self.

1. Reflect on Your Current Identity: Take time to reflect on the various roles you play in life (e.g., the "successful professional," the "perfect parent," the "stoic friend") and identify which of these are ego-driven identities. Write down the false identities you have adopted in response to fear, shame, or the desire to protect yourself.
2. Explore the Roots of These Identities: For each false identity, consider where it came from. What fear or wound was it protecting? How has it served you in the past, and how is it limiting your growth now? Explore the emotional and psychological benefits these identities have provided and how they continue to reinforce avoidance.
3. Create a New Self-Description: Now, write a new, more authentic self-description. This description should reflect your true values, desires, and emotional needs, without the layers of protection or masks you have adopted. Focus on the qualities that align with your soul's truth—compassion, vulnerability, authenticity, and self-acceptance. Your new self-description should feel empowering and aligned with who you are at your core.

4. Affirm and Embody: Once you've written your new self-description, commit to embodying it in your daily life. Notice when the old ego-driven identities resurface and gently remind yourself of the authentic self you are choosing to embrace. Over time, this practice will help you move from ego-driven behavior to soul-driven choices, allowing you to live with greater freedom, authenticity, and connection.

CHAPTER 4

THE WORTHINESS WOUND: MAKING THE UNCONSCIOUS CONSCIOUS

Trauma doesn't just hurt in the moment; it leaves invisible scars on how we see ourselves. Carl Jung famously said, "Until you make the unconscious conscious, it will direct your life, and you will call it fate." This idea sits at the heart of Avoidance is Suicide. The patterns we refuse to face—our deepest wounds, fears, and shame—continue to shape our choices, relationships, and self-perception, whether we realize it or not. The worthiness wound, that deep-seated belief that we are not enough, operates in the shadows, fueling cycles of self-sabotage, unhealthy coping mechanisms, and a desperate search for external validation.

Avoidance keeps these wounds alive, reinforcing the illusion that we are powerless to change. But when we turn inward and begin the work of self-inquiry, we strip away the unconscious control these wounds have over us. Making the unconscious conscious is not just about awareness—it is about reclaiming the power we unknowingly surrender to past pain. It is the first step toward breaking free from the patterns we mistake for fate.

For years, I unconsciously internalized the abuse I experienced as proof that I was unworthy of love, protection, or care. I carried the weight of shame and took on the burden of my father's actions and all the other past abuse that was not my choice, on my shoulders. I tried pretending that everything was ok. But it certainly wasn't. In doing so, I was almost abusing myself. I engaged in relationship dynamics that mimicked secrecy, and I learned to expect betrayal and to not vocalize my needs. I ended up in patterns of failed relationships, relationships that at bear minimum involved poor communication and emotional/physical unavailability and at times, sexual violence. I was with a boyfriend who told me he did not care that I did not feel like having sex, and I gave in and gave up on myself instead of trying to escape that situation, even though it felt wrong. I was not conscious of it at the time, but I was trying to mask my shame, while also normalizing betrayal.

If I somehow pretended I was ok with it, it would hurt less, and it would give me hope that I can maybe find love in this man. After all, with the level of awareness I had at the time, I was attracted to the guy and wanted it to last. If I could somehow make the impossible possible, that would rid me of my shame. Similarly, if the relationship with a long-distance or emotionally unavailable partner would work, somehow that would make me good enough. I did not know it at the time, but what I was trying to do was to repair what was broken in me through looking to others to save myself, while also inviting the same exact dysfunction and thus making it impossible to integrate those broken parts of myself, as I was breaking them even more. I was in a vicious cycle and unaware of it. I know now that I was calling it fated love, but really what it was is my unhealed worthiness wound attracting dysfunctional emotional dynamics that felt familiar, like the version or lack of love I had experienced and mimicked the past. And those I was looking towards to make things right, were not the right people, because they were also unhealed, unaware and in their own cycles, so there was no chance of things working out. I was in a perpetual cycle of self-sabotage and self-betrayal.

After my mother's passing, my father's actions, coupled with his refusal to acknowledge the truth, left me questioning my value as a person. When I finally confronted him after my mother's death, his response shattered me. He called me 'crazy' to other family members, in the hopes of preserving his image, while weaponizing the pain he inflicted upon me against me. It did not matter if I was the one with the PhD in psychology. I was crazy according to them and had lost my mind. My brother's betrayal and choice to take my father's side after I shared what had happened reinforced the narrative that my voice didn't matter, that I didn't matter. Any hope I had about him acknowledging what he had done, died as well. It was now very clear that I had to stop hoping for something that would never come. The acknowledgment that I was looking for on the outside had to be given to me by me.

What was very different is that by the time this happened, I was much more aware than I had ever been in my life. I was left feeling completely alone in the world but was able to take the time to reflect as all of this was happening. I had to fight incredibly hard to find my worth from within, which was the greatest blessing, but also one of the most painful periods of my life. Eventually, I built an immense amount of inner strength, the kind that is unshakeable, because it was derived from within. This time, I was not afraid of confronting and feeling my pain and seeing things for what they are, no matter how uncomfortable it was.

The Power of Awareness: How Bringing Unconscious Thoughts, Emotions, and Patterns to Light Empowers You to Heal

At the core of healing and personal transformation lies the profound and often overlooked power of awareness. Awareness, in the context of psychological and emotional healing, is not merely an intellectual acknowledgment of thoughts and feelings but a deep, embodied understanding of their presence, origin, and impact. The unconscious mind, which comprises a vast reservoir of repressed memories, unresolved emotions, and automatic behavioral patterns, functions outside the realm of our conscious awareness. While this system has evolved to protect the self from emotional pain, it simultaneously perpetuates unresolved trauma, avoidance, and self-sabotage.

Making the unconscious conscious refers to the deliberate process of bringing these repressed or hidden aspects of the psyche into conscious awareness. This process is not about merely intellectualizing or labeling emotional experiences, but about deeply engaging with them, understanding their origin, and transforming them into a conscious, integrated part of the self. The act of uncovering unconscious thoughts, emotions, and patterns opens the possibility for deep healing. It allows individuals to break free from automatic reactions and avoidance behaviors, gaining the agency to choose healthier responses to life's challenges.

The power of awareness lies in its capacity to interrupt the perpetuating cycles of reactivity and avoidance. When unconscious patterns are brought to light, individuals no longer have to blindly follow the directives of the ego or the trauma-induced defense mechanisms. Instead, they are empowered to make conscious, informed decisions that reflect their authentic desires, needs, and values. By making unconscious material conscious, one can dismantle the power of trauma and shame, reclaim self-worth, and engage in healthier, more adaptive behaviors.

However, this process requires both patience and vulnerability. The unconscious mind is often resistant to change, as it is intricately tied to survival mechanisms and defensive strategies. Confronting unconscious patterns often evokes discomfort and fear, as it demands emotional courage and the willingness to face unresolved pain. Nevertheless, this confrontation is not merely a path to self-knowledge, but a powerful vehicle for transformation, enabling individuals to reclaim their personal power and create new, more empowering narratives about their lives.

The Subconscious Mind: Understanding How Your Subconscious Mind Shapes Your Beliefs, Actions, and Avoidance Behaviors

The subconscious mind is a vast and intricate network that governs much of our thoughts, feelings, and behaviors, operating primarily beneath the surface of conscious awareness. While the conscious mind processes immediate, present experiences and decision-making, the subconscious mind holds our core beliefs, early childhood experiences, emotional conditioning, and ingrained responses to stressors. This vast, hidden territory is not merely a passive repository of memories but a dynamic influence on how we experience the world and respond to it.

Central to understanding the subconscious mind is recognizing that it plays a pivotal role in shaping our beliefs about ourselves and the world. From a young age, individuals internalize messages, both explicit and implicit, that shape their sense of self-worth, identity, and belonging. These beliefs are often formed in response to early trauma, attachment wounds, or societal conditioning. For instance, an individual who experiences emotional neglect in childhood may develop a subconscious belief that they are unworthy of love, creating a deep-seated fear of rejection that continues to influence their relationships throughout adulthood.

These subconscious beliefs operate as automatic filters, determining the way we perceive and react to situations. A person who subconsciously believes they are unworthy of success may unconsciously sabotage opportunities for achievement, while someone with a subconscious fear of failure may avoid taking risks or pursuing their passions. Such behaviors are often perceived as self-sabotage, but they are in fact the result of subconscious patterns that are aimed at protecting the individual from perceived threats, even if those threats are no longer present.

The subconscious mind also plays a central role in avoidance behaviors. When individuals experience emotional discomfort or distress, the subconscious mind activates defensive mechanisms to shield them from further harm.

These mechanisms may include dissociation, numbing, denial, or withdrawal. While these strategies may have been adaptive in past experiences of trauma or emotional pain, they become maladaptive when they prevent the individual from engaging with present challenges in healthy ways.

The key to healing and transformation is to become aware of these subconscious patterns, which often manifest as recurring thoughts, emotional triggers, and avoidance behaviors. Once brought to light, these patterns can be examined, understood, and reframed, enabling individuals to release their hold over the psyche and replace them with conscious, empowered choices.

Tools for Making the Unconscious Conscious: Mindfulness, Meditation, Inner Child Work, and Body Awareness as Tools for Self-Discovery

Several practices can be employed to facilitate the process of bringing unconscious material into conscious awareness. These tools help individuals access deeper layers of the psyche and engage with emotional material that may otherwise remain repressed or hidden. While no single tool is a cure-all for addressing all unconscious patterns, a holistic approach that integrates multiple techniques can create a powerful container for self-discovery and healing.

1. Mindfulness: Mindfulness is a practice of focused, non-judgmental awareness in the present moment. By cultivating mindfulness, individuals can begin to observe their thoughts, emotions, and physical sensations without becoming attached to them or reacting automatically. This observational stance creates space between stimulus and response, allowing individuals to interrupt habitual, unconscious patterns of avoidance or reactivity. Over time, mindfulness helps to sharpen self-awareness and allows for a more conscious engagement with the present moment, without the filter of past trauma or subconscious fear.

   Mindfulness can be particularly helpful in identifying unconscious patterns as they arise in daily life. For instance, an individual may notice feelings of anxiety, defensiveness, or irritability in response to certain situations. Through mindfulness, they can explore the underlying beliefs and emotions that fuel these reactions, thereby increasing their capacity to respond with greater awareness and intentionality.

2. Meditation: Meditation, particularly techniques like insight meditation or focused attention, provides a deep,

reflective space in which individuals can access unconscious material. By quieting the mind and cultivating inner stillness, individuals can create a receptive environment for uncovering suppressed memories, beliefs, or emotions. Meditation enables the practitioner to explore the depths of their subconscious, providing insights into the origins of their avoidance behaviors and helping to reframe the beliefs that underpin them.

In addition to its role in self-awareness, meditation also helps to regulate the nervous system and cultivate a sense of emotional equilibrium. This is especially important when confronting challenging or painful material, as it helps to ground the individual in the present moment, preventing overwhelming feelings from overtaking their awareness.

3. Inner Child Work: Inner child work involves connecting with and healing the younger parts of oneself that may have experienced trauma or emotional neglect. These aspects of the self often hold unconscious beliefs and emotional patterns that shape current behaviors. By accessing the inner child through visualization, dialogue, or journaling, individuals can engage with the emotional

wounds of the past and offer compassion, comfort, and healing to these parts of themselves.

Healing the inner child is essential for reclaiming self-worth, as many individuals carry subconscious beliefs rooted in childhood experiences of shame, rejection, or neglect. Re-parenting the inner child through self-compassion and nurturing can begin the process of reprogramming these deep-seated beliefs and healing old emotional wounds.

4. Body Awareness: The body is often referred to as the "unconscious mind," as it holds and expresses repressed emotions, traumas, and unresolved psychological material. Techniques such as somatic experiencing, body scanning, and breathwork help individuals reconnect with the sensations in their bodies, which may reveal areas of emotional blockage, tension, or discomfort. Through somatic practices, individuals can access the physical manifestations of unconscious emotional pain and begin to release them.

Body awareness is particularly powerful because it allows individuals to bypass the cognitive, ego-driven mind and engage directly with the emotional experience stored in the body. This somatic approach helps individuals reconnect with their inherent vitality, grounding them in the present moment and facilitating emotional healing through physical release.

Through mindfulness, meditation, inner child work, and body awareness, individuals can uncover and integrate the unconscious patterns that have shaped their lives.

Practical Exercise: Daily Mindfulness Practice to Uncover Unconscious Patterns and Reactions

To begin the process of making the unconscious conscious, the following daily mindfulness practice can be utilized. This practice helps individuals uncover the hidden patterns, emotional triggers, and avoidance behaviors that influence their responses to life's challenges. By incorporating daily mindfulness into your routine, you begin to create a bridge between the unconscious and conscious mind. With consistent practice, you will develop the ability to observe your thoughts, emotions, and bodily sensations with greater clarity and compassion, allowing for deeper self-awareness and the conscious release of avoidance behaviors. By making the unconscious conscious, you empower yourself to break free from the chains of trauma, shame, and avoidance, reclaiming your emotional and psychological freedom.

1. Set an Intention for the Day: Each morning, set an intention to remain mindful and aware of any unconscious patterns or emotional triggers that may arise throughout the day. This intention helps prepare the mind to engage with situations consciously, rather than reacting automatically.
2. Mindfulness of Thoughts: As you move through your day, observe your thoughts without judgment. Notice when automatic, negative, or self-limiting thoughts arise. These thoughts may point to deeper subconscious beliefs or emotional wounds. Pause for a moment to reflect on the origin of these thoughts and whether they reflect your true values and self-awareness.
3. Mindfulness of Emotions: Throughout the day, check in with your emotional state. Notice any recurring emotions—such as anxiety, anger, sadness, or defensiveness—that may arise in response to certain triggers. Instead of suppressing or reacting to these emotions, simply observe them with curiosity and compassion. Ask yourself: What are these emotions trying to teach me? Where do they originate from?
4. Body Awareness: At various points during the day, take a few moments to scan your body for any area of tension,

discomfort, or tightness. These physical sensations often correlate with emotional blockages or unresolved trauma. By breathing into these areas and gently releasing tension, you can increase body awareness and facilitate emotional release.

5. Reflect at the End of the Day: At the end of each day, take time to reflect on your mindfulness practice. Write down any insights or patterns that emerged. Did you notice any unconscious behaviors or emotional reactions? What can you learn from them? How can you apply this newfound awareness in the future?

CHAPTER 5

THE PARADOX OF FACING PAIN: HOW TRAUMA SHAPES OUR RELATIONSHIPS

Pain, particularly emotional pain, often represents one of the most formidable barriers to personal healing and growth. It is an undeniable truth that the confrontation of pain—whether it manifests in the form of trauma, grief, or unresolved psychological wounds—elicits profound fear. However, paradoxically, it is through the very process of confronting these emotional afflictions that individuals can experience profound personal transformation. This chapter explores the complex dynamics of facing pain, the psychological underpinnings of the fear of healing, and the potential for growth through emotional confrontation.

For many years, I carried the belief that I was unworthy of love, and being that I had experienced a relationship between my parents where my mother was left to raise us by herself, and my father was physically and emotionally absent, I also believed that love means I will be alone, even while in a relationship. This belief, planted by the violations I endured as a child and young adult, became the lens through which I saw myself and the relationships I was involved in. I gravitated toward partners who mirrored the dynamics of emotional or physical unavailability, control, manipulation, deception, betrayal, and disregard that I had internalized from my early life. These relationships were abusive, a cycle of pain that I couldn't seem to break, especially because every time I met someone who reminded me of those dynamics, I thought it was "meant to be."

At the time, I didn't understand that I was unconsciously drawn to what was familiar, even if it hurt me. The relationships reinforced my feelings of shame and inadequacy and kept me stuck in the narrative that I wasn't good enough for real love or respect. Each failed relationship deepened the wound, and I found myself repeating the same patterns, hoping for a different outcome but unwilling to face the underlying causes of my choices.

This cycle wasn't just about the relationships themselves; it was about my avoidance of the deeper pain I carried. I was not fully aware of it at the time, but it felt easier to focus on external conflicts than to confront the internal ones. But as the years passed, the weight of these experiences became too much for me to ignore, and with my mother's passing, my whole world turned upside down, the pain of losing her was unbearable, and with it, all the hidden pain I had in me rose to the surface. My mother's passing was a catalyst to facing my pain.

The Fear of Facing Pain: Why Confronting Your Deepest Fears Feels Impossible but Is the Key to Healing

The human mind is often wired to avoid pain, whether physical or emotional, as a protective mechanism. From an evolutionary standpoint, this avoidance strategy served as a critical survival tool, steering individuals away from potentially dangerous or harmful situations. However, when applied to emotional pain, this instinctual avoidance creates a paradox. While the mind seeks to avoid suffering, the refusal to confront deep-seated emotional wounds only prolongs and exacerbates the very suffering it seeks to avoid.

Psychologically, the fear of facing pain is rooted in various mechanisms, including the activation of defense mechanisms such as repression, denial, reaction formation, rationalization, projection, and dissociation. These mechanisms serve to shield the individual from overwhelming emotional distress. However, their long-term effect is the entrenchment of emotional numbness, wherein the individual becomes disconnected from both painful and positive emotional experiences. This disconnection prevents the natural process of emotional processing and growth, leaving individuals in a state of stagnation or emotional suppression and most likely wearing a mask.

The challenge lies in the paradox of confronting emotional pain: the very act of facing one's fears appears unbearable, yet it is this confrontation that unlocks the potential for healing. As Carl Jung said, "What you resist not only persists, but will grow in size." This insight underscores the truth that avoidance only amplifies the intensity of emotional pain, and pushes one further away from healing, while maintaining an alienating false sense of self, which ultimately makes the individual a stranger to themselves. Individuals may fight to preserve the false sense of self due to fear of the unknown and what happens if they dare to look within. By engaging with and processing painful emotions, individuals are given the opportunity to integrate their experiences, creating a sense of coherence and psychological resilience. The journey is not easy, but the relief and sense of contentment that result from this process makes it worth it.

Plato's Allegory of the Cave: Trapped in a False Reality, Mistaking Shadows for Truth

Plato's allegory of the cave illustrates how individuals can be trapped in a false reality, mistaking shadows for truth because it is all we have ever known. The prisoners in the cave resist enlightenment, clinging to the familiar illusions even when presented with the possibility of a greater reality. This resistance mirrors the struggle we face when we become alienated from our true selves, holding tightly to a false self-image constructed from societal expectations, past trauma, and internalized shame.

For many of us, the false self serves as a protective mechanism—a carefully curated identity built to avoid discomfort, rejection, or pain. It provides a sense of stability, even if that stability is rooted in illusion. Like the prisoners in the cave, we may actively fight against anything that threatens our constructed identity, fearing the unknown more than the suffering we have normalized. To step out of the cave, to challenge long-held narratives about who we are, means confronting uncertainty and, often, deep emotional wounds.

But refusing to leave the cave has a cost. By preserving the false self at all costs, we remain strangers to our authentic nature. We may experience a persistent sense of emptiness, anxiety, or self-doubt without fully understanding why. Our unconscious wounds continue to drive our choices, keeping us trapped in cycles of avoidance, unfulfilling relationships, and self-sabotage. True healing requires the courage to turn toward the light—to dismantle the illusions, face the discomfort of transformation, and step into the unknown. Only then can we reclaim our true selves, free from the shadows that once defined us.

This theme is woven into many modern stories, perhaps most famously in The Matrix. Neo's journey is a direct parallel to the challenge of making the unconscious conscious. When faced with the truth—that the world he knows is an illusion—he is given a choice: take the red pill and see reality for what it truly is or take the blue pill and return to the comfort of his fabricated existence. Like Neo, we all face this decision in our own way. We can continue living within the limits of our conditioned beliefs, numbing ourselves to deeper truths, or we can choose to wake up. But awakening comes at a cost—it means leaving behind the identity we once clung to, questioning everything we thought we knew, and stepping into uncertainty.

The cost of refusing to see is even greater. When we avoid the truth, we remain prisoners to our unconscious wounds, allowing them to dictate our behaviors, habits, relationships, careers, and ultimately our self-worth. We become stuck in repetitive cycles, never fully understanding why we feel disconnected or dissatisfied. We convince ourselves that our suffering is just the way things are, mistaking survival for living. But when we choose to wake up—when we make the unconscious conscious—we reclaim our power. We stop being passive participants in our own lives and start becoming the authors of our own stories.

Embracing Pain as a Path to Growth: How Facing and Processing Emotional Pain Leads to Personal Transformation

The confrontation with emotional pain is not an end in itself but a means toward achieving a state of greater psychological integration and wholeness. Research in the field of emotional processing and trauma therapy highlights the notion of "post-traumatic growth," a phenomenon in which individuals report experiencing significant personal growth following the active processing of trauma and pain. This process of growth is multifaceted, often encompassing greater emotional resilience, increased empathy, a deeper sense of purpose, and a redefined sense of self.

Central to the concept of embracing pain is the idea of emotional integration. Emotional integration refers to the process of acknowledging, experiencing, and ultimately assimilating painful emotions into one's broader narrative of self. This process can be thought of as a form of emotional alchemy—transforming raw, unprocessed suffering into a more manageable and, in some cases, enlightening experience. By allowing oneself to sit with pain and process it in a safe, structured environment, individuals can begin to deconstruct the power that pain holds over them, thus gaining mastery over their emotional states.

Moreover, the act of embracing pain can facilitate a deeper understanding of one's psychological patterns and underlying beliefs. The work of Virginia Satir suggests that emotional pain often stems from unmet needs or deeply ingrained beliefs about oneself, others, and the world. Through confronting pain, individuals are provided with the opportunity to challenge and reframe these beliefs, leading to personal growth and a more adaptive way of engaging with the world. In this way, pain becomes a catalyst for transformation, rather than an obstacle to growth.

The Fear of Healing: Why We Fear Healing and Change, and How to Push Through That Fear

Despite the potential for growth, the process of healing is often accompanied by a profound fear of change. Change, even when it promises relief or improvement, is inherently destabilizing. For many individuals, the fear of healing is intertwined with the fear of the unknown. Emotional wounds, even those that cause significant distress, can become familiar and comfortable over time. In some cases, individuals may identify with their pain or use it as a means of coping with other aspects of their lives. For example, a person may unconsciously cling to their victimhood or trauma narrative because it provides a sense of identity or purpose, or because it serves as an explanation for certain life struggles.

The fear of healing is also tied to the broader human resistance to vulnerability. Healing often necessitates emotional exposure—allowing oneself to be vulnerable and acknowledging one's weaknesses and limitations. The discomfort associated with vulnerability is a central theme in the works of Brené Brown, who emphasizes the transformative power of embracing vulnerability as a pathway to courage, creativity, and connection. However, for many, this vulnerability is perceived as threatening, leading to resistance or avoidance of the healing process.

Additionally, the process of healing often requires letting go of familiar but maladaptive coping mechanisms, such as emotional suppression or avoidance. For some individuals, these coping strategies have become ingrained patterns of behavior, and the prospect of change can be daunting, especially when we are not fully aware of these mechanisms or how to approach our healing process. The fear of losing these mechanisms, even if they are ultimately harmful, can impede progress in the healing journey.

To push through the fear of healing, it is essential to cultivate self-compassion and a willingness to embrace discomfort as part of the transformation process. As mindfulness-based approaches to therapy suggest, the key to overcoming fear lies in developing a mindful awareness of the present moment, allowing individuals to acknowledge and accept their fears without being controlled by them. Through the practice of mindfulness, individuals can learn to reframe their relationship with fear and pain, seeing them as temporary states rather than permanent conditions.

Practical Exercise: Guided Visualization to Safely Confront and Begin Healing Your Most Painful Memories

For individuals seeking to initiate the process of healing, a guided visualization exercise can provide a safe and structured environment in which to confront and process painful memories. The following exercise is designed to help individuals begin the process of emotional integration and healing through mindful engagement with their emotional pain. By practicing this visualization regularly, individuals can begin to confront their emotional pain in a safe and controlled manner, fostering a sense of empowerment and agency in the healing process.

Step 1: Creating a Safe Space. Find a quiet, comfortable place where you will not be disturbed. Sit or lie down in a relaxed position. Close your eyes and take several deep breaths, allowing your body to relax with each inhale and exhale. Visualize a peaceful, safe space—this could be a place you have been to before or an imagined sanctuary where you feel completely at ease. Allow this space to serve as a mental refuge, a safe container for any emotions or memories that may arise during the exercise.

Step 2: Identifying the Source of Pain. Bring to mind a painful memory or emotion that you wish to address. It may be helpful to start with a less overwhelming experience, gradually working your way up to more difficult memories. Allow the memory to come to the forefront of your awareness. Notice any physical sensations or emotions that accompany the memory. Do not attempt to change or suppress these sensations; simply observe them with curiosity and acceptance.

Step 3: Engaging with the Pain Now. Visualize yourself in the presence of the pain or memory, but within the safe space you have created. Imagine that you can interact with the memory, observing it as though it were an image or story unfolding before you. Allow yourself to feel any emotions that arise but do so from a place of compassion and understanding. Acknowledge the pain without judgment, recognizing that this emotion is a part of your experience but does not define you.

Step 4: Offering Compassion. As you engage with the painful memory, imagine yourself offering compassion to the younger version of yourself who experienced the pain. Picture yourself offering comfort, understanding, and love. This act of self-compassion can begin to soften the emotional intensity of the memory, creating space for healing and integration.

Step 5: Reframing the Narrative. Finally, consider how you might reframe the memory. Rather than seeing it as a source of suffering, try to view it as part of your broader journey of personal growth. Reflect on what you have learned from this experience and how it has shaped you. Embrace the possibility that healing is an ongoing process, one that will unfold in its own time.

The paradox of facing pain lies in the fact that the very act of confronting our emotional wounds, which seems unbearable at first, is the key to healing and personal transformation. While the fear of pain and the fear of change may initially block our progress, it is through embracing and processing these experiences that we achieve psychological resilience and growth. By cultivating a willingness to face our pain, engaging in mindful practices of self-compassion, and reframing our narratives, we can navigate the complex terrain of emotional healing and emerge more integrated, whole, and empowered.

CHAPTER 6

THE COLLECTIVE INFLUENCE OF SOCIETY

Society, in its broadest sense, plays an insidious yet profound role in shaping the individual psyche. It establishes norms, values, and expectations that often conflict with the authentic self. These societal structures impose an implicit framework for what it means to be "successful," "worthy," and "acceptable." As individuals, we are conditioned to meet these external standards, which, while providing some measure of stability, often come at the cost of our own sense of truth and identity.

Consider how societal constructs like success, appearance, and conformity create unrealistic expectations. The drive to fit in, to adhere to norms that privilege wealth, status, and perfection, leads to a deep sense of inadequacy in those who feel they fall short. This collective programming forms the core of much internalized shame—the silent force that perpetuates avoidance behaviors. The more we fail to align with the narrow confines of what society deems acceptable, the greater the sense of "less-than" that permeates the individual psyche.

Shame as a Tool of Control

The role of shame within the societal framework cannot be overstated. Cultural narratives that emphasize perfectionism, productivity, and the acquisition of status and material wealth form the underpinnings of modern shame. This shame is not just an individual phenomenon but is socially constructed, reinforced through media, advertising, and social channels that magnify feelings of inadequacy, comparison, and self-judgment. These externalized standards create a profound sense of disconnection, where individuals, particularly those who do not conform to these ideals, experience a deep sense of being "unworthy." One setting where this is profoundly influential is the workplace, where those who challenge the status quo or voice dissenting opinions often find themselves marginalized, overlooked, or even penalized, as conformity is frequently valued over critical discourse. This leaves individuals feeling alienated and at odds with themselves as they are now in a predicament where they must keep working in a setting where they are not valued. Paradoxically, unless awareness is brought into this topic, the very individuals who promote and perpetuate this structure are the ones who are also entrapped by it, often at the cost of creativity and productivity.

This sense of inadequacy at the individual level is often exacerbated by the incessant bombardment of idealized images of success in the media and on social media platforms. The curated portrayal of flawless lives and bodies creates an environment in which the individual feels perpetually behind, exacerbating feelings of shame and self-loathing. As these pressures mount, avoidance becomes a natural coping mechanism, shielding the individual from the emotional pain that arises from such societal comparison. The interplay between societal pressures and internalized shame fosters a culture of avoidance that prevents genuine healing and self-acceptance.

Avoidance as a Survival Mechanism in Society

The temptation to avoid pain through external means is ever-present in a society that encourages instant gratification. I was no exception to this. Whether through emotional numbing or seeking external validation, I resisted the discomfort of facing my true feelings. Yet, every attempt to avoid the discomfort only prolonged my suffering. I used research, work, and relationships to avoid sitting with the very real pain I was carrying inside.

Throughout my studies, and afterwards my daily 9-5 routine, burying myself in tasks that distanced me from my emotions—kept me from truly confronting my emotional wounds. It wasn't until I recognized these avoidance mechanisms for what they were that I began to break free from their hold. The key to healing lay not in evading the discomfort but in learning to sit with it and process it in a way that empowered me, rather than keeping me trapped in disconnection.

I began to slowly let go of the walls I had built. I chose to allow myself to heal rather than continue the cycle of numbing. In doing so, I not only began to heal myself but also opened the door to helping others do the same. I no longer allowed fear, shame, or societal expectations to dictate the course of my life.

Avoidance, in many respects, functions as a survival mechanism within modern society. In a culture that prizes emotional numbness, instant gratification, and the suppression of discomfort, individuals are encouraged—whether overtly or subtly—to avoid experiencing the full spectrum of emotional pain. This avoidance manifests in various forms, including excessive busyness, substance use, social media engagement, workaholism, gambling, overeating, undereating and consumerism among others. The increasing reliance on external distractions to numb emotional pain is a direct reflection of the societal aversion to vulnerability and emotional depth.

This cultural narrative of "toughening up" and "moving on" compels individuals to reject their emotional pain as something weak and unworthy of attention. The constant emphasis on "getting over it" without addressing the underlying trauma fosters a climate where true healing is sidelined in favor of superficial coping mechanisms. While these behaviors may provide temporary relief, they do not address the core emotional wounds, leading to deeper disconnection from the authentic self and perpetuating the cycle of avoidance.

The Rat Race: A Never-Ending Cycle of Striving and Avoidance

The rat race is a metaphor for the relentless, competitive pursuit of success, wealth, and social status, often at the expense of personal fulfillment, well-being, and individuality. It describes a cycle in which individuals feel compelled to work harder and achieve more, yet find themselves perpetually dissatisfied, as the goalposts of success continually shift.

In a society that prioritizes comparison and glorifies unattainable standards—whether in career, appearance, lifestyle, or material wealth—people become trapped in the rat race by constantly measuring themselves against unrealistic ideals. Social media, corporate culture, and societal expectations fuel this cycle, reinforcing the belief that one must always be more—more productive, more successful, more perfect. This external validation becomes the driving force behind decisions, leading individuals to sacrifice their passions, mental health, and even personal values in pursuit of an illusion.

The trap deepens as people equate self-worth with external achievements, fearing that slowing down or stepping outside conventional success metrics means failure. Breaking free requires a fundamental shift in perspective—redefining success on one's own terms, disengaging from comparison-driven validation, and prioritizing meaning over societal approval.

In contemporary society, the so-called "rat race" epitomizes the relentless pursuit of success, external validation, and achievement. In this context, success is often narrowly defined by material wealth, professional accomplishments, and social status. The intense pressure to excel and outpace one's peers creates a pervasive sense of inadequacy, as individuals tie their sense of self-worth to external accomplishments. This creates a fertile ground for avoidance, as individuals seek refuge in distractions that promise relief from the dissonance between their true selves and the demands of the world.

In this sense, the "rat race" is the very embodiment of societal pressure. It tells us that our value is determined by our accomplishments—our ability to climb the ladder, achieve success, and prove our worth to the world. In a society that breeds complacency, no one questions the very foundations on which these notions are built, and we all continue to play along. I also played along, working tirelessly, achieving accolades, but never truly feeling fulfilled. The more I achieved, the more I felt disconnected from myself, and that is because I was not in alignment with my authentic self. The pressure to constantly perform, to "do more," only created an environment where self-worth was tied to external validation rather than inner fulfillment.

In my own life, this race was marked by a series of pursuits that were never enough. I kept striving for success, hoping that the recognition I sought would fill the void of the emotional disconnection I felt throughout the rest of my life. But no amount of external achievement could heal the trauma that lived within me. The more I chased external rewards, the more I distanced myself from the core of who I was. While my career path involved something true to me, the disconnect lay in the lack of integration of what I was learning with my personal life and past pain. In fact, the study of psychology for a while meant that I was as good as the number of papers I published, etc.

The rat race not only stifles personal authenticity but also leads to profound emotional and physical exhaustion. The chase for success, while seemingly noble, often results in burnout and a pervasive sense of emptiness. As individuals devote themselves to meeting arbitrary benchmarks of success, they risk losing touch with their core values, desires, and purpose. This disconnection from self becomes the ultimate irony: in pursuit of success, individuals often lose the very essence of what makes them feel truly fulfilled.

This lens shifts in a fundamental way if the accomplishment or the endeavor is aligned with one's true purpose. If the individual, coming from a place of awareness and authenticity, chooses their life and career path based on their values and desires, the journey becomes more meaningful and worth the sacrifice.

Overmedicating: A Coping Mechanism That Disempowers

As society increasingly turns to quick fixes to address emotional pain, overmedication has become a prevalent form of avoidance. The pharmaceutical industry's growing influence and the normalization of medication as a solution for anxiety, depression, and emotional distress reflect a broader societal trend toward disempowerment. While medications may offer temporary relief from emotional discomfort, they do not address the root causes of the pain and instead push the individual further away from healing. Overmedication has become the business-as-usual model of behavioral health, where medication is offered way before therapy, if at all. This perpetuates a cycle of dependency, where individuals feel disconnected from their ability to self-regulate their emotions or face their pain head-on.

In modern psychiatry and behavioral health, overmedication has become the norm, often prioritizing symptom management over true healing. The current system, heavily influenced by Big Pharma, encourages quick pharmaceutical fixes rather than addressing the root causes of psychological distress. This over-reliance on medication alienates individuals from their own healing process, reinforcing the belief that their struggles are purely biochemical rather than influenced by trauma, environment, and deeper emotional wounds.

A key driver of this issue is the Diagnostic and Statistical Manual of Mental Disorders (DSM), which has evolved into a tool that medicalizes nearly every aspect of human experience. While originally designed to classify mental health conditions for research and treatment, the DSM has increasingly become a means of pathologizing normal emotions, leading to overdiagnosis and excessive prescriptions. The danger of misdiagnosing individuals is significant—many who suffer from unresolved trauma, existential distress, or spiritual crises are instead labeled with disorders that justify medication rather than deeper therapeutic intervention.

Big Pharma profits enormously from this cycle. The more diagnoses exist, the larger the market for psychiatric drugs, leading to a system where medication is the first, and often only, solution offered. Meanwhile, patients who could benefit from therapy, holistic interventions, or lifestyle changes are led to believe they are permanently broken, dependent on prescriptions to function. This model not only distances individuals from true self-awareness and empowerment but also perpetuates long-term dependency rather than healing.

Breaking free from this system requires a shift in focus—one that acknowledges the complexity of mental health beyond biochemical imbalances. True healing demands a more integrative approach that includes trauma-informed care, holistic wellness, and self-exploration, rather than the passive acceptance of a pill as the only answer.

Overmedication offers the illusion of control, as it might initially appear to provide a temporary sense of relief;

however, it ultimately contributes to a deeper sense of disempowerment of individual and society collectively. The overfocus on symptom management, not only in the world of Western medicine but also through certain therapeutic approaches that never scratch the surface other than offering "coping skills" draw a low ceiling that prevents individuals from engaging with their emotional landscape authentically. The disconnection from the true self that arises from this reliance on external substances, which also carry side effects with implications for physical health, and build tolerance, fosters a continued state of avoidance, which only serves to reinforce the cycle of trauma, avoidance and shame. This poses the fundamental question: Is the behavioral healthcare system structured in a way that truly empowers the individual? If you are a clinician, are you contributing to this structure?

The Disconnection from the True Self

In a society that continually reinforces the ego as the measure of success, many individuals experience a profound disconnection from their authentic selves while struggling to fit in or live up to impossible standards. This disconnection is not simply a personal issue, but a societal one, as external pressures force individuals to suppress emotions, desires, and authentic expression in order to conform to established norms. The ego thrives in this environment, promoting external validation and the pursuit of status at the expense of deeper emotional truths.

The price of this disconnection is significant: individuals who fail to connect with their true selves experience feelings of emptiness, burnout, and a lack of fulfillment. The constant pressure to conform to societal expectations fosters a sense of identity that is inauthentic and fragmented. In this context, the process of reconnecting with the authentic self becomes a radical act of defiance—a rejection of the ego's false image and a reclaiming of one's true essence.

In a culture that elevates the ego, authenticity becomes a marginalized concept. Society's obsession with external achievements, appearances, and status places the ego at the forefront of personal identity. The ego thrives in environments where vulnerability is suppressed, and conformity is rewarded. This creates a paradox: individuals are encouraged to prioritize the image they project to the world over the deeper, more authentic aspects of their identity. As a result, authenticity becomes an act of resistance, one that requires the courage to step outside the boundaries of societal approval and embrace the truth of one's inner experience.

When Rebellion Becomes Another Cage

In our current culture, many of the loudest movements are framed as liberation — a way to reject oppression and reclaim identity. But often, what's paraded as "woke" is really a rebellion against shame, not a resolution of it. It's the psyche's way of saying, I will never let you make me feel small again, while still being entirely controlled by the very wounds it claims to have transcended.

When we have not yet healed, our rebellion can become another mask. We wear it to demand recognition, to force the world to see us in the way we wish we could see ourselves. And while this may be a necessary stage for some — a waystation on the road to authenticity — it is not the destination. At best, it is a loud declaration that we are done being silent. At worst, it is another performance for approval, still tethered to the shame it tries to defy.

Cancel culture is a prime example of this loop. It often begins as an attempt to hold people accountable, but when fueled by unhealed shame, it becomes a mirror of the very systems it wants to dismantle — public shaming, moral hierarchy, exile. Instead of breaking chains, it forges new ones. Instead of unity, it creates division.

Even in wellness spaces, self-righteousness can be just another costume. The "I'm vegan," "I take these supplements," "I only eat clean" proclamations can be rooted in genuine health choices — or in the same subtle power play as any other status symbol. It's another way of saying, I am good because I am doing it right — a moral hierarchy disguised as virtue. True healing is quieter. It doesn't need to announce itself or prove its worth. It moves us beyond rebellion into something deeper: a place where we are no longer defined by what we are against, but by who we truly are.

When Body Positivity Turns Against the Body

There is a difference between loving yourself as you are and demanding the world celebrate choices or conditions that are destroying you. Somewhere along the way, "body positivity" morphed into "body entitlement" — a cultural script where any suggestion that health matters is labeled as oppression.

Representation matters. People of all sizes deserve dignity and respect. But when we plaster every billboard and runway with plus-size models without also talking about the very real health risks tied to obesity, we are not just normalizing bodies — we are normalizing disease. We are pretending that biology is political, that metabolic illness can be shamed into irrelevance if we simply declare it beautiful enough times.

This is not liberation. It is another form of avoidance. Instead of facing the hard truth — that real self-love includes caring for the vessel you live in — we rewrite the narrative, so we never have to change. It is the same shame loop, just painted in pastel colors and hashtags about empowerment.

True health does not come from conforming to a thin ideal or flaunting an "any size is healthy" badge. It comes from honesty. From saying, I deserve love now — but also, I deserve to feel well, live long, and treat my body with care. Anything less is just another costume shame wears to the party.

On the other hand, while individuals are routinely shamed for carrying weight, the larger food ecosystem often escapes scrutiny. Highly processed products, sweetened, salted, dyed, and "fortified" with flavors, are marketed as "comfort," "treats," or "cheat days," normalizing patterns that disconnect us from our bodies. Meanwhile, the upstream realities of industrial agriculture and manufacturing, pesticide-dependent supply chains, additives, and aggressive marketing, are buffered by complex regulations and lobbying that keep consumers focused on willpower instead of systems. This is not an invitation to blame people for what they eat; it is an invitation to see avoidance operating on two levels: collectively, when we avert our gaze from how food is produced and sold to us, and personally, when we use food to numb, reward, or belong in the absence of deeper care.

Agency begins with awareness: questioning the messages that shape our cravings, noticing when "convenience" becomes self-abandonment, and choosing the most nourishing option available, while also asking harder questions of the structures that profit from our disconnection.

The Path to Reclaiming Your Authenticity in a Society that Shames and Avoids

Reclaiming authenticity involves integrating the inner self with the role we play in society. It means finding harmony between the demands of external expectations and the need to stay true to one's essence. Setting boundaries with societal pressures is crucial in maintaining this equilibrium.

True success is not derived from external validation but from the peace and fulfillment that arise from living in alignment with one's core values.

So here is the question: Is your identity a mask, or your truth?

Sometimes the identities we adopt are not born from our deepest self — they are born from wounds. Is your identity your truest expression, or is it a mask you are wearing because it feels safer than facing what is underneath? Rebellion can become a shield against shame: If I shock you, you can't reject me. If I rebel against the way you shamed me, you'll have no choice but to love me for who I am. Just like when I was vulnerable and powerless, now you have no choice but to accept me — or I will organize against you and give you a taste of your own medicine.

Choosing from this place might feel like freedom, but for some it's a way to avoid the vulnerability of facing the wound and processing the pain it hides. Early harm, such as childhood abuse, can shape what we choose, desire, fear, or reject, and how we show up — without us even realizing it.

Only you can know the truth about your choices. This is about noticing when your identity is built as armor rather than as truth. There is a difference between living from your deepest, truest self and living from your survival. Ask yourself: Is this who I am, by choice, when I am living according to my truth, or who I became to survive? Am I stuck in reclaiming what was taken from me? Am I repeating unhealed patterns?

Beyond the Mask

If you find that you are wearing a mask, just know that it is okay to become aware of that — and it is that awareness that eventually frees you from having to wear it. You are not the mask you have been wearing. You are not the performance, the rebellion, or the protection you have built to survive. Those things have served you. They have kept you alive, hidden, safe — but they are not the whole of you. You are older than your wounds and deeper than your defenses. Beneath them lives something older, wiser, and untouched by shame. A self that has never needed to prove anything to anyone. That self is still here, waiting for you to remember. Waiting for you to take off the mask — not because you are exposed, but because you are finally free from the limitations that the mask imposed. The mask kept you alive. Your truth will set you free. You were never meant to be just the version of you that survived. You were meant to live as the version that thrives — the version that does not need to self-betray, beg, please, shock, rebel, or demand love to prove its worth.

Practical Exercise: Integrating the Inner and Outer Self

The journey to authenticity is not a rejection of society but a reimagining of how we interact with it. As we integrate the inner and outer self, we create space for a new way of being in the world—one that is grounded in authenticity, emotional depth, and self-compassion. This is the path to healing, not only for the individual but for society as a whole. The hope is that the practical exercise below will help you to begin to integrate the inner and outer self. As you discover things about yourself, remember that the purpose is to raise awareness to a new level, from a place of self-compassion rather than criticism. With awareness comes choice, and you can eventually begin to pave the road ahead for your journey, one step at a time.

- Breaking the Chains of Societal Conditioning: Reflect on the societal beliefs and expectations that you have internalized. How have these beliefs shaped your decisions and sense of self-worth? Write about how they have influenced your life choices and your personal narrative.
- Reclaiming Your Power: Challenge these societal norms. Write an empowering affirmation that reflects your

authentic values, unclouded by external pressures. How can you begin to live in alignment with your deeper truth?

- Reevaluating Success: Define success on your own terms. What does it mean to live authentically in a world that often prioritizes external achievements over personal fulfillment? How can you redefine success to reflect your inner values?
- Releasing Dependency: Explore the areas where you have relied on external substances or behaviors to avoid discomfort (e.g., medication, alcohol, food, gambling, sex, social media, or anything that you do to avoid facing what you fear). Reflect on healthier, more empowering ways to cope with emotional pain.

CHAPTER 7

BREAKING FREE FROM THE CHAINS OF THE PAST

Becoming a therapist was a dream I had always pushed aside. I told myself it wasn't the right time, or that it wasn't the right career path, but the truth was deeper. I avoided stepping into a role that demanded I confront others' pain because I hadn't yet confronted my own. The thought of sitting with someone else's trauma felt unbearable when I was still running from my own pain. For years, I avoided not just the profession, but the process of healing itself. I told myself that I was fine, that the past didn't matter, that I could move on without revisiting the darkest corners of my life. But avoidance doesn't erase pain—it amplifies it. My unresolved wounds seeped into every area of my life, from my relationships to my self-esteem.

It wasn't until I began to do the work of facing my shadows that I realized the power of vulnerability when it comes to confronting pain, shame and avoidance cycles. Becoming a therapist meant that once I was able to break the cycle of avoiding and fearing and being ashamed of my pain, I would be using my experiences and my years of training in psychology, which in the past had remained completely unintegrated, to help others find their own path to healing.

The past, especially traumatic experiences, can often cast long shadows over an individual's present and future, shaping their identity, their relationships, and their capacity to experience joy and success. While the experience of trauma is inescapable for many, its long-lasting effects on an individual's sense of self-worth, their relationships, and their potential for personal growth can be profound and debilitating. This chapter delves into the connection between unresolved trauma and self-worth, the process of releasing past emotional burdens, and the transformative power of forgiveness as a means to reclaim one's agency and emotional freedom.

The Connection Between Trauma and Self-Worth: How Unresolved Trauma Keeps You from Feeling Deserving of Love, Success, and Happiness

The intersection of trauma and self-worth is deeply embedded in psychological frameworks, such as attachment theory and the concept of relational trauma. Early attachment experiences, particularly those involving neglect, abuse, or emotional unavailability, can lead to the internalization of beliefs that one is unworthy of affection, care, or attention. Over time, these beliefs can crystallize into pervasive feelings of inadequacy, unlovability, or a sense of being "broken." These core beliefs may prevent the individual from seeking healthy relationships, pursuing personal goals, or accepting love and success when they arise, because they feel fundamentally undeserving of these positive experiences.

Trauma, whether physical, emotional, or psychological, can disrupt not only an individual's emotional equilibrium but also their fundamental sense of self. According to trauma theory, the impact of adverse experiences can manifest in lasting cognitive, emotional, and physiological changes that interfere with an individual's ability to fully engage in life. At the core of this disturbance often lies a deep-seated erosion of self-worth. This occurs because trauma, particularly when unresolved, can create maladaptive beliefs about the self, the world, and one's worthiness of love and success.

Furthermore, trauma can often impede an individual's ability to set healthy boundaries and assert their needs. The internalized belief of being unworthy of care can lead to the neglect of one's own needs in favor of others, often reinforcing cycles of self-sacrifice and self-erasure. This pattern is reinforced by maladaptive coping mechanisms such as dissociation, emotional suppression, or hyper-vigilance, all of which are designed to avoid or mitigate the emotional pain of trauma but ultimately reinforce the belief of personal inadequacy.

In contemporary therapeutic approaches, including those influenced by the works of researchers like Bessel van der Kolk and Peter Levine, there is growing recognition of the necessity of addressing these deeply embedded beliefs in the process of healing. Trauma-informed care stresses the importance of validating the individual's experience while providing the tools to reconstruct a healthier, more adaptive sense of self-worth. By confronting and processing the trauma, individuals can begin to dismantle the negative self-concept that has been built around it and begin to rebuild a more resilient and self-compassionate sense of identity.

The Courage to Let Go: How to Release Past Pain, Blame, and Guilt That Hold You Back from Embracing Your True Potential

Letting go of past pain, particularly the emotional residues of trauma, is often perceived as one of the most difficult aspects of healing. The emotional and psychological burden of holding onto pain, blame, or guilt can be paralyzing, and many individuals find themselves caught in cycles of rumination and self-recrimination. However, releasing these emotional weights is not only essential for healing but is also an act of courage that opens the door to personal growth and empowerment.

The psychological concept of "holding on" to past pain can be seen as a form of emotional attachment to a narrative of victimhood or suffering. According to psychoanalytic theory, particularly the work of Melanie Klein and later Donald Winnicott, individuals may develop unconscious attachments to early experiences of pain or loss, which they use as a basis for their sense of self. These attachments often manifest in unconscious ways, such as in the form of chronic self-doubt, depression, or anxiety, and can prevent individuals from embracing the present moment and moving forward into the future.

The emotional process of "letting go" requires both the ability to recognize and acknowledge the grip of past pain, as well as the willingness to release it. This process involves a gradual disentanglement of the self from the traumatic narrative, which allows the individual to redefine their sense of identity. Furthermore, letting go is intricately connected to the notion of acceptance. Acceptance, as defined in Acceptance and Commitment Therapy (ACT), does not mean condoning past actions or resigning oneself to a life of suffering, but rather it involves embracing the present moment with openness and curiosity, while simultaneously releasing the hold of past emotional wounds.

Letting go also involves disengaging from self-blame or the desire to find fault in oneself or others for past events. In the case of trauma, many individuals struggle with feelings of guilt or responsibility, believing they could have prevented the event or that they are in some way to blame for the suffering they endured. This cognitive distortion is known as self-blame and is commonly found in those who have experienced abuse, neglect, or loss. The path to healing, however, involves recognizing that the pain was not deserved, and that the responsibility for healing lies in the hands of the individual, not in the responsibility for the traumatic event. Also, if the individual was not fully aware of the grip their past had on them, on their choices and actions, it is not fair to oneself to self-blame for making those choices. Some may argue that they were aware, but still did things they did not feel good about. Even then, entering the process of forgiveness does not mean that you are not accepting the impact of wrongdoing. It means that you are opening up a pathway to acknowledging how and why you hurt yourself and others and gradually begin to let go of that pain that might be associated with self-loathing or loathing for others, while exercising self-compassion from a place of heightened awareness that you may not have had before.

Forgiveness as Freedom: How Forgiveness (of Yourself and Others) Is Key to Healing and Reclaiming Your Power

Forgiveness, both of oneself and others, is often presented as a key component in the process of psychological healing. While forgiveness has traditionally been viewed as a moral or ethical imperative, contemporary therapeutic approaches underscore its role as a tool for emotional liberation. The act of forgiveness—when practiced with sincerity and genuine understanding—can facilitate the release of deeply held grudges, anger, and resentment, allowing the individual to reclaim their emotional power and autonomy.

The concept of forgiveness has been explored in psychological literature through various lenses. Enright and the Forgiveness Project, for example, assert that forgiveness is not about condoning or forgetting the wrong done but about releasing the emotional hold that the offense has over the individual. Forgiveness is framed as a process of reframing one's emotional response to the injury in a way that shifts the focus from victimhood to empowerment. In this sense, forgiveness becomes a way to free oneself from the chains of anger and resentment that keep an individual tied to their past trauma.

From a psychological perspective, forgiveness is also intimately connected to self-compassion. In the context of self-forgiveness, individuals often struggle with feelings of shame, guilt, or self-reproach for perceived failures or mistakes. Self-forgiveness, however, requires individuals to cultivate a non-judgmental and compassionate view of themselves, acknowledging their imperfections without condemning their inherent worth. This process is central to healing, as it allows individuals to free themselves from the emotional prison of self-criticism, enabling them to move forward with a greater sense of personal agency and self-love.

Moreover, forgiveness is not only a way to release past emotional baggage but also a way to disrupt the cycles of trauma. In the case of forgiving others—particularly perpetrators of trauma—this process is not about excusing harmful behavior but rather about reclaiming one's own power and emotional sovereignty. The work of forgiveness in this context is not for the perpetrator's benefit, but for the individual who seeks to break free from the psychological patterns established by the trauma.

Practical Exercise: A Forgiveness Letter-Writing Ritual to Release Emotional Weight

For individuals seeking to embark on the journey of forgiveness, one effective tool is a letter-writing ritual that facilitates emotional release and self-liberation. The following exercise guides the individual through the process of writing letters to both themselves and others, enabling them to confront and process feelings of anger, blame, guilt, and regret.

Step 1: Preparing for the Ritual

Find a quiet and private space where you can focus without distractions. Take several deep breaths to center yourself and allow any tension in your body to release. You may choose to light a candle, play calming music, or engage in any other activity that helps you enter a reflective and meditative state.

Step 2: Writing a Letter to Yourself

Begin by addressing a letter to yourself, acknowledging any guilt, shame, or anger you may be holding. Write freely and without judgment. Express the pain you feel, the mistakes you think you have made, and the ways in which you have been hard on yourself. Once you have written the letter, read it aloud to yourself, offering words of compassion and understanding. Recognize that you are worthy of forgiveness and that you are not defined by your past mistakes.

Step 3: Writing a Letter to Another

Next, write a letter to someone who has hurt you. This letter is not intended to be sent but is a cathartic exercise to release feelings of anger, resentment, or betrayal. Express how their actions impacted you and the emotional pain they caused. Allow yourself to feel the full extent of the emotions associated with this relationship, and once the letter is complete, offer yourself the choice to release these feelings. You may choose to read the letter aloud or burn it as a symbolic act of letting go.

Step 4: Closing the Ritual

End the ritual by sitting in silence and taking several deep breaths. Reflect on the emotional release you have experienced and acknowledge the courage it took to engage in this process. Recognize that the act of forgiveness is a continual practice and that, with time, you can return to this exercise as many times as necessary to further release emotional weight.

Breaking free from the chains of the past requires not only the courage to confront unresolved trauma but also the willingness to let go of past pain, blame, and guilt. In the process of healing, individuals must navigate the complexities of self-worth, emotional attachment, and forgiveness. Forgiveness, both of oneself and others, offers a profound pathway to reclaiming personal power, releasing emotional burdens, and embracing the full spectrum of human potential. By undertaking the process of emotional release, individuals can forge a new relationship with their past, one that enables them to move forward with greater freedom, self-compassion, and resilience.

CHAPTER 8

RECLAIMING YOUR TRUE SELF

The journey to reclaiming one's true self is a profound and transformative process that requires deep self-awareness, courage, and a commitment to personal growth. For many individuals, the path to authentic selfhood has been obscured by layers of societal expectations, familial conditioning, and unresolved emotional pain. These layers often create a false self—a constructed identity that may be at odds with one's deeper sense of self and potential. Reclaiming your true self involves peeling away these layers, awakening to your inherent power, and cultivating a life grounded in self-love, empowerment, and authenticity. This chapter explores the steps necessary for reconnecting with your inner strength, redefining your identity, and establishing the boundaries that will protect and nurture your true essence.

Awakening to Your Power: How to Reconnect with Your Inner Strength, Wisdom, and Authenticity by Letting Go of Avoidance

In many cases, avoidance becomes a habitual response to fear—fear of facing uncomfortable truths, fear of vulnerability, or fear of failure. However, the act of confronting fear is paradoxically the key to reclaiming one's power. Carl Jung's notion of the "shadow" self suggests that the aspects of ourselves we repress or avoid often hold the key to our deepest personal growth. The shadow contains both the disowned parts of our personality, such as unacknowledged strengths or desires, and unresolved traumas that prevent us from living authentically. Psychological avoidance, whether through distraction, dissociation, or denial, is a common defense mechanism used to shield oneself from emotional discomfort or trauma. While avoidance may offer temporary relief, it also perpetuates a cycle of disconnection, preventing individuals from accessing the full range of their emotional and psychological resources.

Awakening to one's power requires embracing the totality of the self—both the light and the dark, the strengths and the vulnerabilities. This process of integration is central to achieving psychological wholeness and is facilitated by practices such as mindfulness, self-compassion, and deep introspection. By learning to sit with discomfort, rather than avoiding it, individuals can reconnect with their innate wisdom and strength, cultivating an inner resilience that is grounded in authenticity.

The process of awakening is deeply connected to the discovery of one's core values and passions. According to existential philosophy, authentic living is a process of aligning one's actions with one's deepest values, passions, and purpose. This alignment requires individuals to let go of external pressures and societal expectations that may obscure their true desires. The pursuit of authenticity is, therefore, an ongoing journey of self-discovery, self-expression, and self-empowerment. The first step in reclaiming one's true self is to awaken to the power that resides within. This process involves confronting and overcoming the avoidance mechanisms that have kept individuals disconnected from their own strength and authenticity.

Redefining Your Identity: Steps to Build a New Self-Image Rooted in Self-Love, Self-Worth, and Empowerment

For many individuals, the identity they have constructed over the years may be rooted in external validation, societal approval, or past experiences of trauma. These externally imposed identities often fail to reflect the individual's true essence, leaving them feeling disconnected, unfulfilled, or lost. Rebuilding a new self-image requires a conscious effort to dismantle the old, limiting beliefs and replace them with affirming, empowering perspectives that are aligned with the truth of each individual and what they want to embody. Redefining one's identity is a critical aspect of reclaiming the true self.

Self-love is the foundation of a new, authentic self-image. In his work on self-compassion, psychologist Kristin Neff emphasizes that self-love involves treating oneself with the same care, kindness, and respect that one would offer to a loved one. This concept of self-love is not self-indulgence or narcissism, but rather the ability to acknowledge one's intrinsic worth without needing to earn it or prove it to others. It is the recognition that one's value is inherent and unconditional.

Building a new self-image also involves challenging deeply held beliefs about one's worth, particularly those that may have been formed in childhood or because of traumatic experiences. Cognitive-behavioral therapy (CBT) and other therapeutic modalities work to uncover and challenge negative self-talk and cognitive distortions that contribute to a distorted self-image. These cognitive distortions, such as catastrophizing, overgeneralization, or self-blame, often lead individuals to view themselves through a critical or judgmental lens. In contrast, a healthy self-image is rooted in self-acceptance, self-compassion, and an understanding that personal growth is a continuous process.

Self-worth, which is often linked to one's identity, must be cultivated through intentional practices that affirm one's inherent value. This may involve setting personal goals, celebrating accomplishments, and engaging in activities that foster a sense of mastery and competence. Additionally, redefining one's identity requires a willingness to step outside the constraints of social norms or familial expectations. To create an empowered self-image, individuals must be willing to embrace their uniqueness and pursue paths that align with their true desires and capabilities, even when these paths may not conform to conventional expectations.

The work of reframing one's identity is also an act of personal liberation. It involves breaking free from limiting beliefs about what one can or cannot achieve, what one is or is not capable of, and what one deserves or does not deserve. Reclaiming one's identity is ultimately about owning one's narrative, rather than letting external forces dictate it.

Creating Healthy Boundaries: Learning How to Say No and Protect Your Energy from Toxic Patterns and People

One of the most essential aspects of reclaiming your true self is learning how to establish and maintain healthy boundaries. Boundaries are emotional and psychological protections that safeguard one's well-being and sense of self. The ability to set boundaries is central to self-empowerment, as it enables individuals to assert their needs, protect their energy, and prevent the encroachment of toxic patterns or people.

Individuals who have experienced trauma, neglect, or emotional invalidation often struggle with setting boundaries. This difficulty can stem from a history of boundary violations, such as emotional abuse, where one's personal space, feelings, or needs were disregarded or invalidated. As a result, these individuals may have learned to prioritize the needs of others over their own, leading to chronic self-neglect or a pattern of people-pleasing.

Creating healthy boundaries is a critical step in reclaiming personal power. It begins with the recognition that one has the right to protect their emotional and physical space. According to boundary-setting theory, developed by experts such as John Townsend and Henry Cloud, healthy boundaries are necessary for maintaining psychological well-being and cultivating healthy, respectful relationships. Setting boundaries may involve learning to say "no" when necessary, advocating for one's own needs, and removing oneself from situations that are emotionally or physically harmful.

The process of boundary-setting also requires individuals to confront the fear of rejection, conflict, or disapproval. Many individuals avoid setting boundaries because they fear the potential fallout or the loss of relationships. However, as assertiveness training and self-empowerment literature have shown, setting clear and respectful boundaries ultimately leads to healthier, more balanced relationships where both individuals can thrive. Establishing boundaries is not an act of selfishness but of self-respect—it is an essential practice for maintaining one's energy and emotional well-being.

Additionally, boundary-setting involves recognizing and disengaging from toxic patterns and relationships that drain one's energy or perpetuate negative cycles. This may involve distancing oneself from individuals who are manipulative, controlling, or emotionally abusive. Over time, individuals who practice healthy boundaries develop a stronger sense of self, as they are no longer defined by the expectations or demands of others.

Practical Exercise: Writing a New, Empowered Vision of Yourself Based on Your True Potential

A powerful way to begin the process of reclaiming your true self is to write a vision of the person you wish to become—one that is rooted in your authentic potential, self-worth, and empowerment. The following exercise invites you to craft a vision of your ideal self, one that aligns with your deepest desires, values, and strengths.

Step 1: Quiet Reflection

Begin by finding a quiet, comfortable space where you can reflect without interruption. Take several deep breaths and allow yourself to relax into the present moment. Reflect on the qualities that define your true self—those aspects that are intrinsic to who you are, beyond societal expectations or past experiences.

Step 2: Identify Your Core Values

Think about the values that are most important to you. These values may include authenticity, compassion, integrity, freedom, creativity, or any other guiding principles that resonate deeply with you. Write these values down and consider how they inform the person you wish to become.

Step 3: Describe Your Empowered Self

Write a detailed description of your empowered self. Include the qualities you wish to embody, the goals you want to achieve, and the life you want to create. Describe the way you want to show up in relationships, work, and in your own personal journey. This vision should reflect the core of who you truly are, not who you feel you "should" be.

Step 4: Set Intentions and Action Steps

Once you have written your empowered vision, consider the steps you need to take to begin living in alignment with that vision. These steps may involve setting boundaries, pursuing personal goals, or engaging in activities that support your self-worth and growth. Write down concrete actions that you can take in the coming days, weeks, and months to bring this vision to life.

Step 5: Embrace the Journey

Acknowledge that the process of reclaiming your true self is ongoing. Your empowered vision is a guide, not a destination. It is a living document that will evolve as you continue to grow and discover new aspects of yourself.

Reclaiming your true self is a dynamic and transformative journey that involves awakening to your inner power, redefining your identity, and establishing boundaries that protect and nourish your authentic self. By reconnecting with your inherent wisdom and strength, embracing self-love and self-worth, and cultivating the courage to set healthy boundaries, you can create a life that reflects your true potential. This process of reclaiming your selfhood is not a one-time event but an ongoing commitment to living authentically, empowered by the knowledge that you are deserving of love, success, and fulfillment.

CHAPTER 9

LIVING AUTHENTICALLY

Embracing your authentic self is like following the White Rabbit from Alice in Wonderland down the rabbit hole—at first, it feels like chasing something elusive, a curiosity tugging at the edges of your reality. But once you step through, the world as you knew it begins to unravel. The illusions you once believed—about who you are, what you should be, and what truly matters—start to dissolve, revealing a deeper, more chaotic, yet profoundly real version of yourself.

The journey is not neat or predictable. Like Alice, you may question everything, encounter strange and uncomfortable truths, and face parts of yourself you once tried to ignore. But the deeper you go, the more you realize that the madness of authenticity is far more liberating than the carefully constructed mask of the surface world. To follow the White Rabbit is to choose awakening over illusion, self-trust over conformity, and the beautiful, messy truth of who you are over the safe, stagnant comfort of who you were told to be.

Living authentically involves aligning your actions, beliefs, and choices with the deepest truths of who you are. It is the process of shedding the false identities, societal expectations, and ego-driven desires that have obscured your sense of self and stepping into a life that reflects your true essence. Authentic living is not merely an aspirational concept, but a dynamic and evolving state of being that requires ongoing self-awareness, introspection, and courage. At its core, it is about honoring your intrinsic values, passions, and purpose, and allowing them to guide your decisions and behaviors.

Breaking free from patterns of avoidance wasn't easy for me. It required me to sit with emotions I had spent a lifetime running from—grief, rage, shame, guilt and fear. I had to learn to recognize the ways I was sabotaging myself, not only in relationships but in my career and personal growth. Healing was a process of unlearning. I had to unlearn the idea that I wasn't good enough, that I was destined to repeat the pain of my past. I had to unlearn avoidance and replace it with curiosity and compassion. Each step was painful, but each step was also a reclamation of my life.

Healing is not linear, nor is it easy. For years, I avoided the truth of my experiences because facing it felt like standing in front of a tidal wave. But the more I avoided, the more the pain consumed me. It wasn't until I began to sit with my feelings—really sit with them—that I started to reclaim my life. I learned to name my pain. To feel it. To release it. I found tools that worked for me, from mindfulness practices to yoga to therapy, that helped me confront the memories I had buried. Slowly, I began to separate my identity from the trauma I experienced. I was no longer just a survivor; I was a woman reclaiming her power.

Living authentically is not merely a destination but a continuous process of alignment, growth, and self-expression. By cultivating the joy of presence, sustaining your growth through emotional resilience and self-awareness, and engaging in practices that support your authenticity, you create a life that reflects the deepest truths of who you are. This journey requires both commitment and courage, but it offers the possibility of a life that is deeply fulfilling, meaningful, and aligned with your true purpose.

Aligning with Your Purpose: How to Live in Alignment with Your True Self and Pursue Your Passions

To align with your purpose, it is necessary to first cultivate a profound understanding of who you are beneath the layers of conditioning and trauma. This requires deep self-reflection and an examination of the beliefs, experiences, and emotions that have shaped your current sense of identity. Purpose, in this context, is not a fixed goal but a fluid, ever-evolving process that is deeply interconnected with your core values and authentic desires. It emerges when you tap into your innate creativity, intuition, and sense of meaning, and allows you to express yourself fully in the world.

The alignment with purpose is often obscured by the mind's habitual tendencies to seek external validation, avoid discomfort, or protect against past wounds. These defense mechanisms, while adaptive at one point, hinder the ability to live authentically by preventing you from engaging with your true desires and potential. The work of aligning with your purpose involves a deconstruction of these defense patterns and an invitation to step into the unknown—into a life that may feel uncertain but is rich with potential and fulfillment.

This alignment requires not only self-awareness but also the courage to embrace uncertainty and change. The path toward authenticity is not a linear one; it is characterized by moments of doubt, fear, and discomfort. However, by continuously returning to the core of your true self—your passions, values, and vision for your life—you can begin to make decisions that resonate with your deepest truth, rather than reacting out of fear or habit. It is a continual process of recalibration and trust, guided by the knowledge that living authentically is a journey, not a destination.

The Joy of Presence: How Being Fully Present in the Moment Frees You from the Grip of Past Trauma and Future Fears

One of the most significant barriers to living authentically is the tendency to become trapped in the past or the future. The mind, conditioned by trauma and fear, often oscillates between rehashing old wounds or projecting future anxieties. This habitual mental activity keeps you locked in patterns of avoidance, preventing you from fully engaging with the present moment. When you are constantly chained to past pain or future uncertainties, you are unable to experience the fullness of life as it is occurring.

The joy of presence, however, offers a profound antidote to this cycle. Presence is the state of being fully engaged in the here and now, without the distraction of past regrets or future worries. It is about returning to the body and senses, reconnecting with the immediate experience of life, and embracing the richness of each moment without judgment or attachment. When you are present, you are no longer identified with the story of your past trauma or the fears of your future; instead, you become an active participant in the unfolding of your life, open to the possibilities that each moment holds.

The practice of being fully present frees you from the grip of past trauma, which often manifests as lingering shame, guilt, or resentment. Trauma tends to anchor us in repetitive thought patterns that replay past events, reactivating the emotions associated with them. By cultivating presence, you begin to untangle these repetitive thought loops, bringing your awareness back to the current experience and away from the emotional charge of memories. Presence thus becomes a means of emotional liberation—of consciously choosing not to be defined by your trauma but to experience life in its current form.

Similarly, presence alleviates the fear of the future, which often emerges from anxiety, uncertainty, or a desire for control. Fear of the future is rooted in a projection of what might go wrong, often based on past experiences of pain or loss. When you cultivate presence, you engage with life as it unfolds, rather than attempting to control or anticipate what is yet to come. This shift from future-oriented fear to present-oriented engagement helps to release the anxiety that constrains your growth and well-being.

The joy of presence, then, is not just about being in the moment—it is about recognizing the inherent peace and freedom that exists within that moment. It is a practice that allows you to step out of the cycle of avoidance and into the full spectrum of your emotional and sensory experience, reconnecting with the aliveness that is always available to you.

Sustaining Your Growth: How to Maintain Your Newfound Freedom and Continue Evolving Without Falling Back into Avoidance

Transformation is not a one-time event but a lifelong process of evolving into a fuller expression of your true self. Once you have begun to break free from the patterns of trauma, avoidance, and self-sabotage, the challenge becomes sustaining that growth and avoiding a regression into old habits. This requires a deepening of your commitment to self-awareness, as well as the cultivation of practices that support ongoing evolution and healing. Living authentically requires ongoing commitment to personal growth and self-awareness.

To sustain your growth, it is essential to establish and maintain practices that anchor you in your authentic self and keep you aligned with your purpose. These practices serve as tools for emotional regulation, mental clarity, and spiritual nourishment, helping you to stay grounded and connected to your true essence, even when external circumstances or internal challenges arise.

One key aspect of sustaining growth is the cultivation of emotional resilience. Growth often involves confronting discomfort and uncertainty, and it is natural to experience moments of doubt or fear along the way. Emotional resilience is the ability to navigate these challenges without falling back into avoidance or self-sabotage. It involves developing a healthy relationship with your emotions—allowing them to flow through you without becoming overwhelmed or reacting impulsively. Resilience is built through practices like mindfulness, meditation, and self-compassion, which help you cultivate emotional intelligence and the ability to respond to life's challenges with wisdom and equanimity.

Another essential aspect of sustaining growth is the practice of self-reflection and self-correction. As you continue your journey, you will inevitably encounter moments where you feel disconnected from your authentic self or tempted to revert to old patterns. These moments are opportunities for deeper self-awareness and integration. Self-reflection allows you to observe the ways in which you may be unconsciously slipping back into avoidance behaviors, while self-correction involves taking conscious steps to realign with your true values and intentions. This process is not about perfection, but about acknowledging when you've strayed off course and gently returning to your path.

Additionally, it is important to recognize that sustaining growth requires ongoing self-compassion. Healing and transformation are not linear, and there will be times when you encounter setbacks, difficulties, or periods of stagnation. In these moments, it is crucial to treat yourself with the same kindness and understanding that you would offer a loved one. Self-compassion allows you to navigate challenges with grace and resilience, without succumbing to self-criticism or shame.

Practical Exercise: Daily Gratitude and Manifestation Practices to Stay Grounded in Your Authentic Self

To stay grounded in your authentic self and sustain your growth, daily practices of gratitude and manifestation can be powerful tools. These practices help you maintain focus on your true values and purpose, while also fostering a sense of abundance and possibility in your life. Below is a guided exercise that combines gratitude and manifestation techniques to anchor you in the present moment and support your continued evolution. By incorporating gratitude and manifestation practices into your daily life, you cultivate an ongoing connection to your authentic self and your sense of purpose. These practices help you stay grounded, present, and aligned with your true desires, and allow you to continue your journey of growth and transformation without falling back into avoidance or self-sabotage.

1. Gratitude Practice: Begin each day by writing down three things you are grateful for. These can be simple aspects of your life or more profound experiences that have shaped your journey. Gratitude helps to cultivate a positive mindset and keeps you connected to the present moment, reminding you of the blessings in your life. It also serves as

a powerful antidote to fear, scarcity, and avoidance, shifting your focus from what is lacking to what is abundant.

2. Manifestation Practice: Following your gratitude practice, take a moment to visualize your life as it unfolds when you are living in full alignment with your authentic self. Close your eyes and imagine yourself pursuing your passions, feeling fulfilled, and expressing your true essence in the world. What does this look like? What emotions arise as you envision your life? Write down these visualizations and feelings in a manifestation journal. This practice helps to reinforce your sense of purpose and align your thoughts and actions with your deepest desires.
3. Integration into Daily Life: As you move through the day, periodically return to your gratitude and manifestation practices. In moments of stress, doubt, or uncertainty, revisit your gratitude list or visualization to realign with your authentic self. By integrating these practices into your daily routine, you create a continuous thread of connection to your purpose, keeping you grounded in your true essence and focused on your evolution.

CHAPTER 10

THE ROAD AHEAD

The path toward healing and self-actualization is not a singular event but a dynamic, ongoing journey—a process that unfolds over time, often in nonlinear ways. Healing, in its truest sense, is not the eradication of suffering or the attainment of a flawless state of being, but rather the continual process of self-discovery, emotional integration, and growth. It involves an openness to the ebbs and flows of personal transformation, an acceptance of imperfection, and a recognition that every step—whether forward or seemingly backward—contributes to a deeper understanding of the self and a more authentic way of being in the world.

One of the most profound realizations in the healing journey is the understanding that growth is not a finite process. It is easy to become disillusioned when healing does not follow a smooth or predictable trajectory. In a culture that often prioritizes rapid achievement and fixed outcomes, it can be tempting to view healing as a destination—something that can be checked off a list once it is "complete." However, true healing is far more complex and multifaceted than such a view allows. It involves continual self-exploration, adaptation, and integration of new experiences, emotions, and insights as they arise.

The awareness that healing is ongoing also brings with it a sense of self-compassion. It allows for the recognition that setbacks, challenges, and moments of doubt are not failures but integral parts of the healing process. These moments are opportunities for deeper understanding and growth, offering the potential to further refine one's relationship with themselves and the world. By embracing the cyclical nature of growth, one learns to approach the journey with patience, grace, and a willingness to meet oneself exactly where they are, without judgment.

Ultimately, embracing the journey is about releasing the need for perfection and instead committing to a lifelong process of becoming—the constant unfolding of your true self in all its complexity. This perspective fosters resilience, enabling you to navigate the challenges that inevitably arise without losing sight of the greater vision of a life lived authentically and fully.

As you move forward on your journey of healing and self-empowerment, it is vital to take moments to celebrate your progress. The tendency to focus on what is still "lacking" or "unfinished" is a common byproduct of both societal conditioning and the internalized voice of self-criticism. In contrast, the act of acknowledging and celebrating how far you have come fosters a sense of accomplishment and reinforces a positive feedback loop of self-affirmation and growth.

Celebrating progress does not necessarily imply that every challenge has been overcome or that perfection has been attained. Rather, it means acknowledging the incremental shifts, the courageous steps, and the ongoing resilience that has brought you to where you are now. Each moment of self-awareness, each step toward authenticity, and each victory—whether large or small—is a testament to the inner work you have undertaken.

The act of celebration can take many forms: it might be as simple as pausing to reflect on the emotional strength you have shown in the face of adversity, or it may involve specific rituals such as journaling, affirmations, or moments of quiet reflection. Rituals of celebration are not only a way to honor your progress but also a way to deepen the connection to the internal resources you have cultivated. These rituals serve as markers on the path of healing, reminders of the resilience, wisdom, and courage you have accessed along the way.

Additionally, celebrating progress helps to counteract the tendency to diminish or invalidate your achievements. In the face of deep-rooted trauma, it is common for individuals to downplay their successes or minimize their growth. Yet, it is precisely these moments of progress—those moments when you have chosen courage over avoidance, self-compassion over self-criticism, and authenticity over the desire for approval—that are the building blocks of a life well-lived. By consistently celebrating these moments, you cultivate an internal environment that is nurturing, empowering, and deeply supportive of continued transformation.

A Life Beyond Avoidance: The Freedom, Peace, and Empowerment That Comes from Facing Your Fears and Stepping into Your True Potential

A life beyond avoidance is not merely the absence of fear or discomfort, but the conscious decision to face and move through them. Avoidance, while a protective mechanism developed in response to trauma, ultimately limits the fullness of life. It creates a barrier between you and your true potential, and it keeps you trapped in patterns of self-sabotage, disconnection, and fear. The act of facing your fears—no matter how daunting—is what frees you from this internal prison and opens the door to the full range of human experience: love, joy, creativity, and fulfillment.

Stepping into your true potential means embracing the fullness of who you are. It involves moving beyond the confines of limiting beliefs, societal expectations, and the protective armor of avoidance to reveal the most authentic version of yourself. It is the act of claiming your inherent worth, accepting your imperfections, and giving yourself permission to express your unique gifts in the world. This step requires not only inner strength but also profound self-trust—the belief that, despite the vulnerability and uncertainty that may arise, you are capable of handling whatever life presents to you.

This process of stepping into your true potential is inherently empowering. It is an act of reclaiming agency over your own life, of choosing to take responsibility for your growth and healing. It is the recognition that you have the power to create a life that aligns with your deepest values and desires, rather than a life that is being dictated by past wounds or external pressures. Empowerment comes from the awareness that you are no longer held captive by your trauma or fears but that you are capable of creating a future that reflects the best of who you are.

Moreover, living beyond avoidance brings a profound sense of peace. When you face your fears—whether they are fears of failure, rejection, or vulnerability—you release the internal conflict that keeps you in a state of tension and avoidance. Instead of expending energy on protecting yourself from potential harm, you free up space for authentic engagement with life. This peace arises not from the absence of challenges, but from the deep inner knowing that you can meet those challenges with presence, wisdom, and resilience.

A life beyond avoidance is one of authenticity, freedom, and joy. It is a life in which you are no longer tethered by the limitations of fear, shame, and avoidance but are empowered to create, love, and be fully present with the unfolding journey of your life. It is a life that recognizes both the beauty and the messiness of being human, and one that chooses to embrace it all with compassion and courage.

CONCLUSION

As you continue your journey of healing, it is important to remember that the road ahead is not defined by a linear progression but by the continual unfolding of your authentic self. Each step, no matter how challenging, is a vital part of the process. The road ahead may not always be smooth, but it is rich with opportunities for growth, self-discovery, and empowerment.

By embracing the journey, celebrating your progress, and living beyond avoidance, you move closer to a life of true freedom and peace. You step into your authentic self and reclaim the agency to shape your life. The road ahead may be filled with twists, turns, and unexpected detours, but with each step, you will find that you are more resilient, more empowered, and more aligned with the truth of who you are.

Healing and transformation, though profoundly liberating, are not always embraced or celebrated by the world around you. As you embark on your journey toward reclaiming your true potential, it is essential to recognize that this path may require you to stand against the current of societal expectations. In a world driven by external measures of success, material wealth, and achievement, stepping onto a road of authenticity and self-healing may seem radical, even unpopular. Society often promotes the pursuit of external validation, quick fixes, and escapism, such as overmedicating, numbing discomfort, or racing through life without truly engaging with the present moment.

Choosing the path of healing may mean opting out of the societal rat race. It may mean rejecting the illusions of safety and security offered by avoidance mechanisms and embracing the discomfort of facing your truth. While this path may feel isolating at times and may even involve sacrificing the approval of others, the reward is an inner freedom that transcends the temporary distractions of societal conformity. You are called to stand firm in your decision to live authentically, even when it is uncomfortable or difficult.

Healing is not just an individual process. As you awaken to your true potential and commit to living authentically, you contribute to a larger, collective shift in consciousness. Healing is contagious; the more individuals choose authenticity over avoidance, vulnerability over defense, and love over fear, the more we collectively transform societal values. When one person heals, it ripples out, creating a larger wave of change. Every small act of courage, every step away from avoidance and into authenticity, has the power to inspire others to do the same.

In this way, your personal commitment to healing and authenticity becomes a catalyst for collective awakening. As you reclaim your true self, you help shift the cultural narrative toward one of deeper connection, emotional honesty, and collective healing. It is through these shifts that we can begin to imagine and build a world where authenticity, compassion, and self-awareness are the norms rather than the exceptions.

Today, I look back on my journey with a mixture of awe and gratitude. What I once saw as insurmountable pain has become the foundation of my purpose. I now understand that avoidance kept me safe for a time, but it also kept me small. By facing all the things that were buried underneath, all the shadows, I found not just healing, but an amazing amount of empowerment, inner strength and relief.

In this book, I draw from my own experiences to help others break free from the patterns of avoidance that hold them back. I know what it's like to feel stuck, to feel unworthy, to feel overwhelmed by the weight of your own story. But I also know what it's like to break through, to step into the light, and to reclaim the life you deserve.

This book is an invitation to you to do the same—to confront the pain, the fear, and the shadows that keep you from living fully. Healing is not easy, but it is always worth it. As I am finishing the last words of this chapter, some of the very concepts I discuss are still challenging to me. I had to grapple with the choice between making an Alias or going by my real name, leaving things out, out of fear of losing my job, or being overwhelmed by shame and fear for sharing personal details, or what the same family members who have declared me "crazy" are going to think and say if I publish this book. I have decided that if I slightly cave in to any of these reservations, shame and avoidance are taking over and will render mute all the points I have tried making in this book.

A Call to Action

Healing is a choice, and it begins with a single step. It is easy to feel overwhelmed by the magnitude of the journey ahead, but remember, the first step toward healing, no matter how small, is a powerful declaration of your intention to live a life free from avoidance, fear, and self-sabotage. Facing fear with courage is not about eliminating fear altogether, but about confronting it with the awareness that it no longer holds dominion over your life. It is about making the decision to live authentically, despite the discomfort, despite the resistance, and despite the uncertain terrain that lies ahead.

Take that first step today. This may look like acknowledging the pain you've been avoiding, or choosing a moment of presence instead of numbing, or reaching out for support. The truth is, your true potential awaits—not in some far-off future, but in the choices you make today. Every moment you choose to show up for yourself, you move closer to a life that is fully lived, aligned with your deepest desires and values. You are not limited by your past, and you are not defined by your fears. You are capable of creating a life beyond your wildest dreams.

Remember, you are never alone on this journey. Even in moments when you feel isolated, know that countless others are walking this path of healing and transformation alongside you. The strength you need to heal and thrive already resides within you. You are not defined by your trauma or your avoidance patterns, but by the resilience, courage, and love you carry within you. Trust yourself. Trust the process. You matter, you are loved, and you are enough. You have the power to rise, to heal, and to become the truest version of yourself.

APPENDIX

RESOURCES FOR FURTHER HEALING

As you continue on your journey of healing and transformation, the following resources may support and guide you in deepening your work:

Recommended Books:

- Loving Them Free by Quynh Lee
- The Body Keeps the Score by Bessel van der Kolk
- Healing the Shame That Binds You by John Bradshaw
- Radical Acceptance by Tara Brach
- The Gifts of Imperfection by Brené Brown

Podcasts:

- The Trauma Therapist Podcast – for resources on trauma healing and growth
- UnFck Your Brain* – for personal empowerment and navigating shame

- The Mindful Kind – for mindfulness practices that help with emotional regulation and presence

Workshops and Therapists:

- Somatic Experiencing Workshops – for trauma healing through body awareness
- Cognitive Behavioral Therapy (CBT) – for challenging and reframing avoidance and unhelpful thought patterns
- Dialectical Behavior Therapy (DBT) – for emotional regulation and self-acceptance

Guided Meditations and Exercises:

- Guided inner child healing meditations to reconnect with the wounded parts of yourself
- Mindfulness meditation exercises for cultivating presence and reducing emotional avoidance
- Self-compassion exercises to build a nurturing, loving relationship with yourself

These resources can further support you as you continue the transformative work begun in this book. Healing is an ongoing journey, but you now have the tools, the insights, and the strength to continue forward with courage, presence, and compassion. The road ahead is yours to navigate, and with each step, you will find greater freedom, joy, and peace.

www.ingramcontent.com/pod-product-compliance
Lightning Source LLC
LaVergne TN
LVHW040519210926
848480LV00007BA/1517
9798349562938